SAILS & SAILING

Dear Dick   1·27·08

Happy Birthday

Love

Antoinette, Joe & Brooke

SAILS & SAILING

A SELECTION OF GREAT NAUTICAL PHOTOGRAPHS FROM MYSTIC SEAPORT'S ROSENFELD COLLECTION

©1998 Fabio Ratti Editoria S.r.l., C.so Monforte 16, 20122 Milano

©1999 Mystic Seaport – Rosenfeld Collection
All reproduction rights reserved.

First U.S. edition October 1999
Second U.S. edition October 2000
ISBN 0-913372-88-9

ITALIAN TEXT
Franco Giorgetti

TRANSLATION
David Steven Talbot

EDITOR
Joe Gribbins

Mystic Seaport Museum, Inc.
75 Greenmanville Avenue
Mystic, Connecticut 06355-0990 USA

Previous Page
The tender to the Vanderbilt family's *Vara* has just disembarked the after-
guard on board *Ranger*, destined to be the last J-class yacht to defend the
America's Cup. Rod Stephens and Olin Stephens are standing to left and
right of Mrs. Vanderbilt. Mrs. Gertrude Vanderbilt, a rare woman crew
member on an America's Cup racer, had an important job aboard *Ranger* –
that of keeping the skipper informed of the adversary's position and move-
ments.

Contents

Cruising

Working

Racing

America's Cup

The *Brenton Reef Lightship*, here undergoing some routine touching up in 1937, was an aid to navigators at the entrance to Rhode Island's Narragansett Bay. Several *Brenton* lightships were on station for over a century from 1853 until 1962.

Thanks to their position marking Brenton Reef, these lightships witnessed some of the most important sailing competitions in the history of American yachting, including America's Cup contests that were sailed off Newport from 1930 until 1983.

Introduction

To speak of sails and sailing vessels is to open a window onto the societies that have sailed them, whether for work or play.

Sailing the sea is an activity born of the contributions of innumerable craftsmen, each a custodian of ancient knowledge and skills. These skills, in turn, are a response to a society's needs, some of them vital, some frivolous – transportation of goods, exploitation of resources, display of status, competition. So photographing sailing yachts and sailing ships is no mere aesthetic exercise. It can be a way to reveal some distinctive features of an entire culture.

This is precisely what the American father-and-son team of Morris and Stanley Rosenfeld have done. For more than a hundred years, almost from when photographic technology first made it possible, and down to our own day, the Rosenfelds have been recording yachts and ships under sail. It is perhaps even more to their credit that they collected important early photographs by some of their contemporaries. This archive of as many as a million images, taken as a whole, is a diverse, exhaustive portrait of a North American sailing culture at work and at play. This unique collection has subsequently been acquired and looked after by Mystic Seaport Museum – with that reverence which the English-speaking peoples have traditionally reserved for the artifacts of their seafaring past.

This book aims to present, by means of a cross-section of the Rosenfeld Collection, the art of sailing as practiced in North America. Toward this end, it has been divided into four chapters. The first three – on working, cruising, and racing – together offer something approaching a systematic overview of the subject. The final chapter, devoted to the America's Cup, may stand as a special homage to the Rosenfelds, since it is to this event they devoted – as Stanley still does – their greatest passion.

The extended notes on each of the pictures do not presume to comment on the images as photography: the intensely communicative photos speak for themselves. Instead, the notes address the role of the images as parts of a story, seeking, insofar as space limitations permit, to express their historic context.

Summarizing his work as a photographer, Stanley Rosenfeld once said, "All I've tried to do is represent the act of sailing as it really is." In my own view, the results transcend the intention, perhaps on account of the complex blending of human and technical factors that sailing always entails. And also, surely, because both the eyes of Stanley and his father have seen and understood with a sensitivity far surpassing that of even the photographic emulsions in which their vision has been – thankfully – fixed forever.

Franco Giorgetti

Cruising

"*N*ever a dull moment."
I can't think of another expression that sums up so happily life
on board a yacht, with all the matchless enthusiasm it arouses.
Sailing just for the pleasure of it is a complex amalgam
of activities, involving both practical concerns
– outfitting, maintenance, handling, navigation –
and poetic immersion in a new world of salt and spray
that liberates us from everyday bonds.
Sailing means harmony with Nature, fresh energy
in both body and spirit, even, in the interactions of a racing
or cruising crew, a transformation of relationships with others.
A pleasure sail is all this and more.
The one thing it never is, never could be, is boring.
Sifting through the photos in this chapter, we spot a common thread.
The boats sail on, and the people sail along with them,
as naturally as can be, with no grand theatrical posturing
– not even when the conditions of wind and water seem highly
unconducive to what we might think of as a pleasurable cruise...

The name of the boat in the photo, *Nedumo*,
is an acronym for the phrase "Never a dull moment."
The words capture the essence both of the picture
and of everything that sailing brings to guests
and crew on a yacht like this.
Nedumo's forty-six-foot length and yawl rig are
perfect for vigorous sailing.
The boat was designed in 1938 by its owner,
who therefore knew it inside and out.
Everything on board looks to be in perfect trim.
The lady in the foreground, a guest on this
breezy day, seems absolutely relaxed.
And definitely not bored.

9

Brown Smith Jones
1935

11
Istalena
1930

13

Valkyrie
1946

Rita Irene
1936

Working

*F*or centuries, the billowing sail meant work.
It was the most efficient source of power for transporting
goods and people, or for going to have a look at
what might be beyond the Pillars of Hercules.
But the gift of wind also exacted a heavy physical
price in human labor. The pictures in this chapter bear witness
to the sweat as well as the romance of the final decades
of commerce under sail. Here, too, is the story
of North American fishing vessels, told in pictures emphasizing
the capacity of these vessels – born of necessity – for speed.
In these images we see a thousand technical details of hulls,
rigging, sail plans. We also come to feel the effort, pain,
and danger of a now-vanished profession, one that deserves
to go unmourned despite the romance we feel,
especially in our very different time, for sailing vessels
and their people. Above and beyond their aesthetic qualities,
the pictures in this chapter are valuable for the technical
and historical information they convey about a world and way
of life that will not come again.
For more than two centuries, from the eighteenth century
through the nineteen-twenties, work and sport had sail
propulsion in common. Since the advent of steam,
and especially since the advent of gasoline and diesel power,
the preservation of sailing traditions and skills has been
the cherished task of those who sail for pleasure.

Launched in 1883, *Tusitala* was one
of the last American wind-powered cargo ships
to leave active service. This 1932 photo shows
the nearly fifty-year-old vessel being towed to
its berth in New York Harbor. While we do not know
what cargo *Tusitala* has taken on board,
the low freeboard tells us that she is fully laden.
It isn't just the lack of wind that makes the tugboat's
presence a necessity. The waters of New York's Lower
Bay were busy and ill-suited for the maneuvers
of sailing ships – and here there's a tide running, too.
Alongside *Tusitala*, a second tug is ready
to help maneuver the big square-rigger.
By the nineteen-thirties, the world's remaining
sailing ships were under heavy pressure
from their steam-powered competitors.
But in this picture not even the tugboat's undoubted
power to help the sailing ship can take away
the majesty of the latter's masts and sails.
Even so, the black smoke, seemingly trying to hide
the rigging, may strike us as a sort of premonition...

17-18
Square-rigger deck
1929

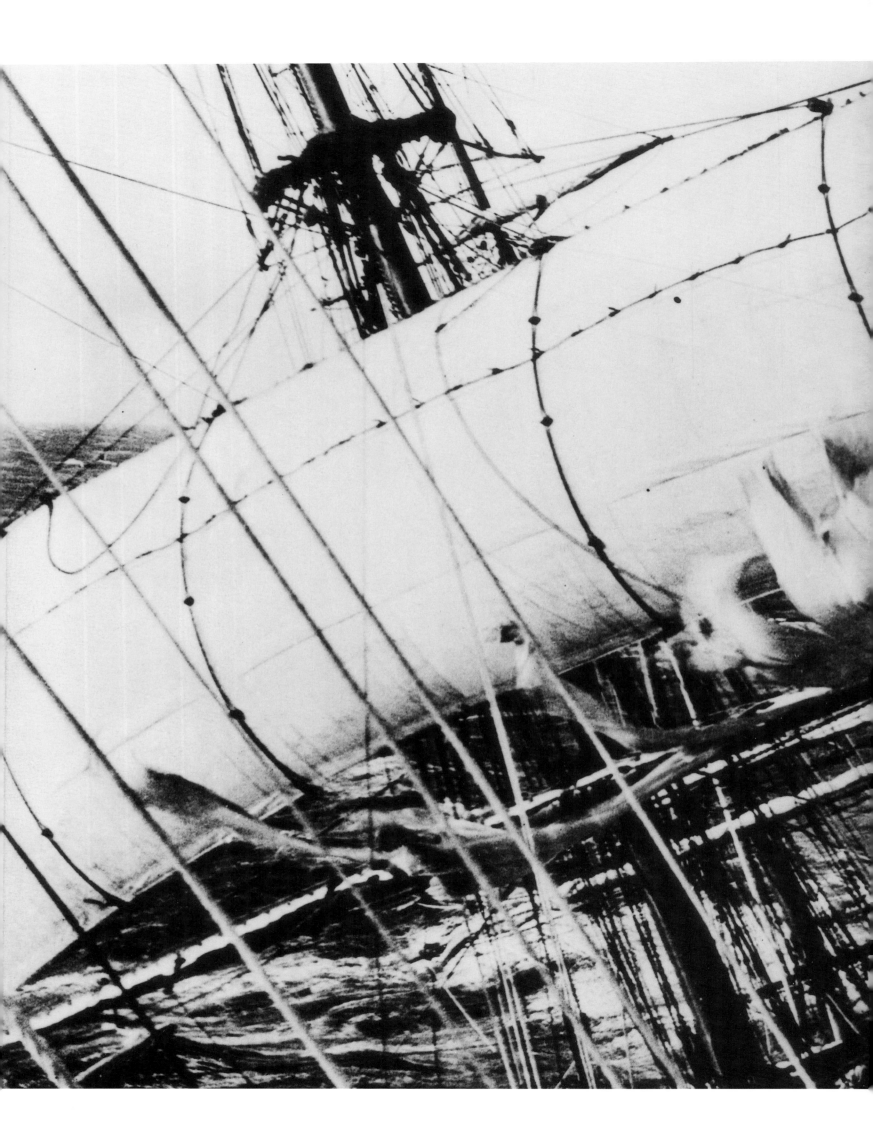

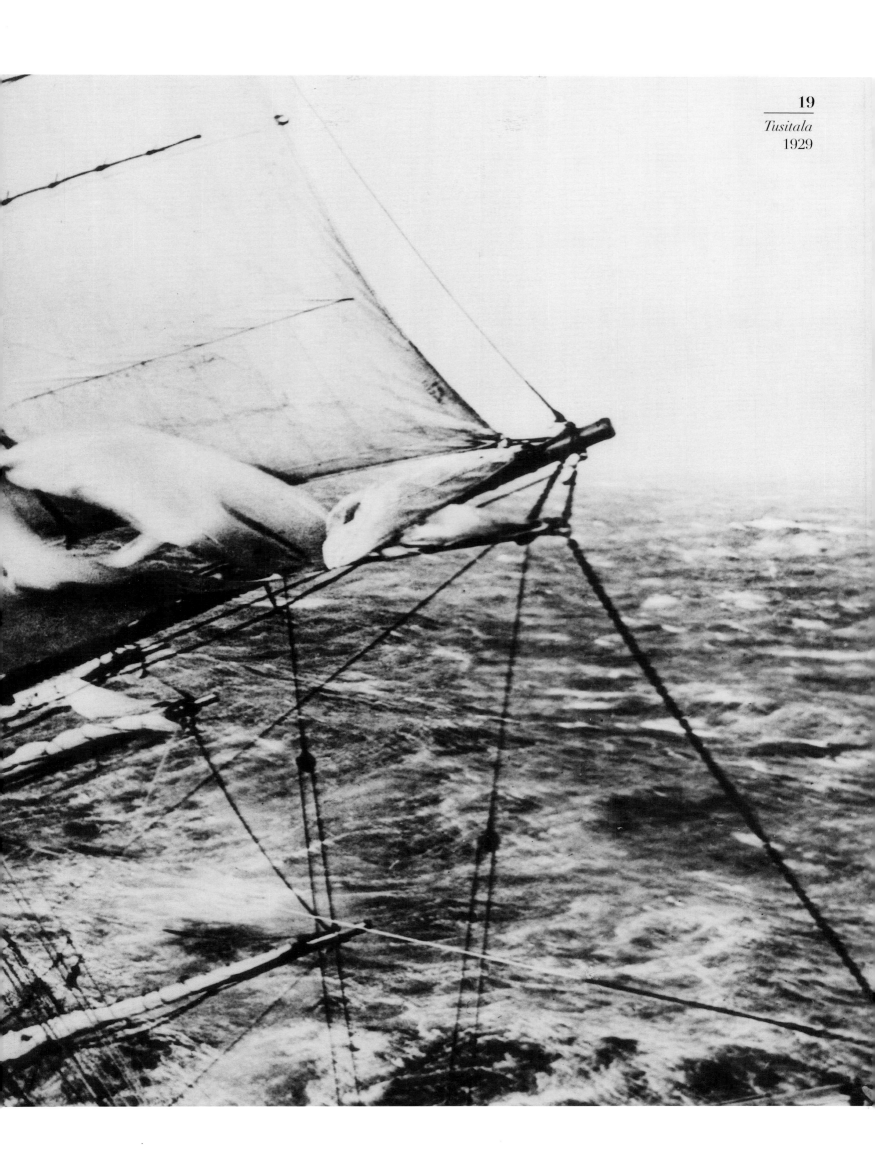

21
Tusitala
1925

22

Seven Seas
1935

25

Henry Ford
1923

26

Robt. Jno. Beswick
1924

27

Splicing rope
1938

Racing

*I*n 1660 a nobleman from Holland, where it was easier
to travel along the waterways than over the few roads,
gave King Charles II of England a "yacht" as a present.
So enthusiastic was the King that he had another sailboat of similar
size and shape built for himself by the then-famous carpenter
Christopher Pett a year later. The King's brother James,
Duke of York, immediately followed suit by ordering a boat
of the same kind from Peter Pett, Christopher's brother.
The first recorded yacht race was the result.
The two yachts competed on the Thames for a purse of one hundred
pounds over a course stretching from Greenwich to Gravesend
and back. For the record, there was no clear-cut winner.
The first part of the race, run against the wind, was won
by the Duke of York's yacht *Anne*; the return leg, before the wind,
saw the Royal yacht *Catherine* – sails billowing,
with the King himself at the helm – overtake its rival.
Surely there were earlier contests among yachts sailed by Romans,
Egyptians, Chinese and other seafaring people – for what sailor,
yachtsman or professional, can resist a race?
Whether carrying tea or wool, clippers tried to reach London
as quickly as they could, literally racing halfway around the world,
since the first cargo unloaded commanded the highest price.
What was more, the clipper making the fastest passage was awarded
a golden windvane; captains were prepared to blow out every sail
they had, one after another, in order to see the coveted prize
glittering at their ships' mastheads.
In the nitrate-exporting ports of Chile, the windjammers
that arrived late had to wait for the others to finish loading
(an operation often taking weeks) before beginning
to do so themselves. Getting there first was thus more
than a sporting proposition.
Races and sails seem to have always gone together.

North American fishermen were so competitive
among themselves that they organized an
international trophy event which continued
to be held for almost twenty years: the Fishermen's
Cup Races. In this photo from the 1938 contest,
the dueling schooners are *Gertrude L. Thebaud*,
an American boat out of Gloucester, and the
Canadian *Bluenose*. The latter had held the title since
1921 and was going to win again this time, too.

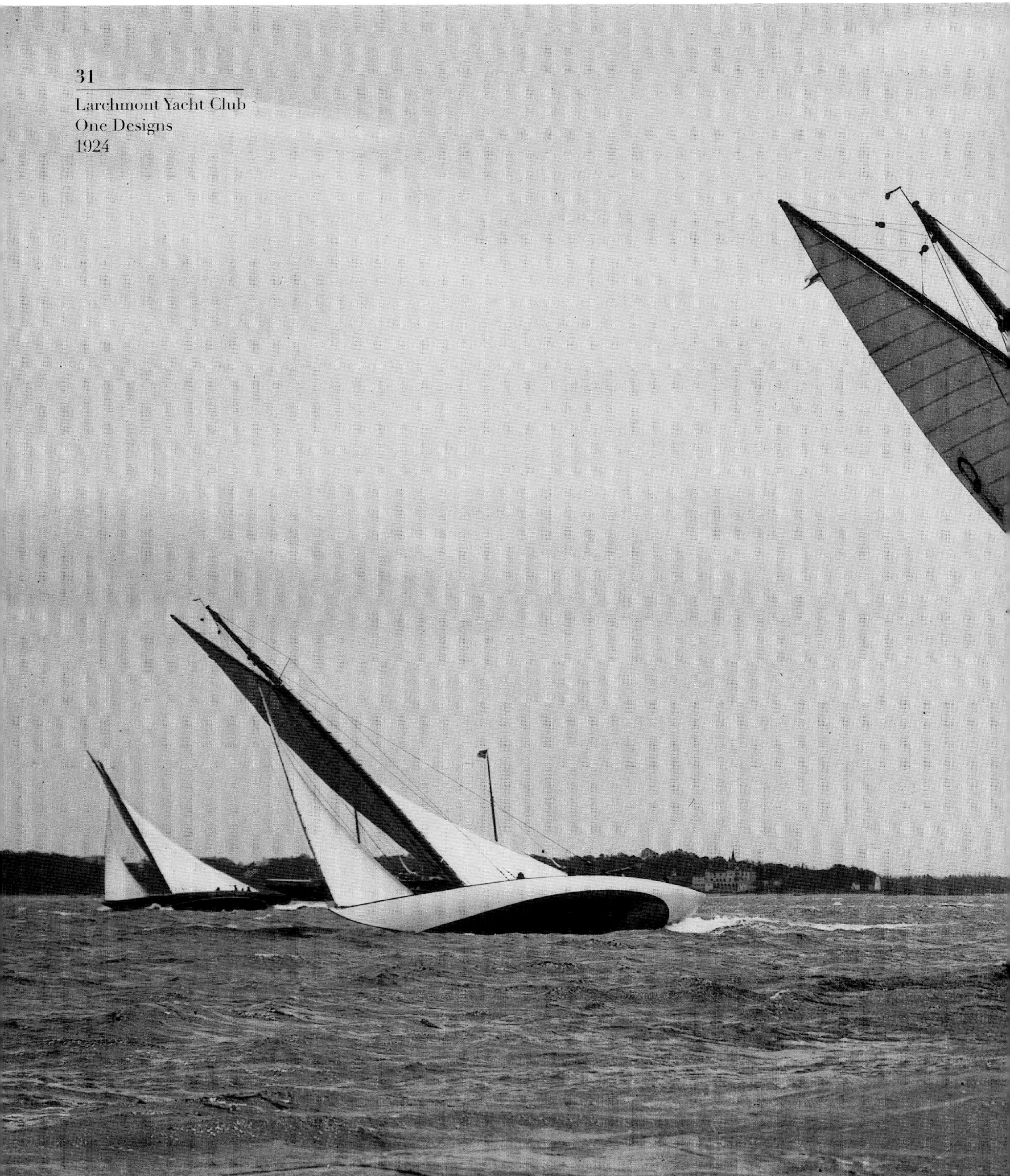

31

Larchmont Yacht Club
One Designs
1924

33

Commodore Nichols
Seawanhaka Corinthian
Yacht Club
1921

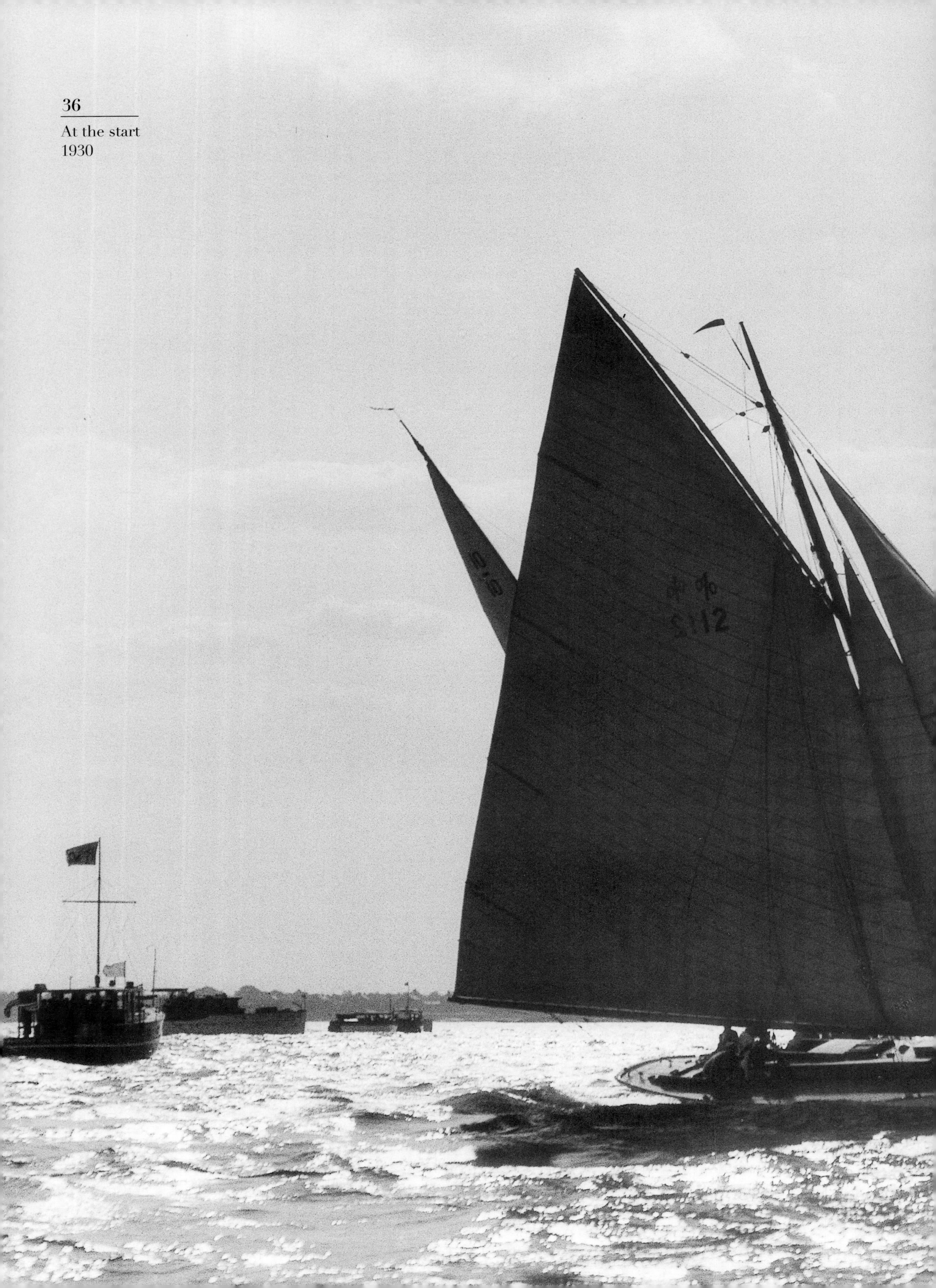

36

At the start
1930

45

Lutine
1952

Ingomar and *Elmina*
circa 1908

Water Gipsy
1936

49

Acushla and *Istalena III*
1921

51
Cotton Blossom III
1941

Tanya II
circa 1950

America's Cup

*I*n 1844 John Cox Stevens and eight friends
– all prominent New Yorkers and sailing enthusiasts –
decided to found a club. Thus did the New York Yacht Club
come into being, and thus, soon enough, a sailing contest
that would capture the imagination of the world.
Six years later, as Commodore of the club, this same J.C.
Stevens decided, together with his brother and three other
members, to challenge the yachtsmen of England.
The schooner *America*, built by Stevens and his syndicate
for the occasion, crossed the ocean, anchored off Cowes
in front of the Royal Yacht Squadron's "castle," and issued
a challenge. The challenge was ignored; but finally *America*
was permitted to enter one of the Squadron's contests.
In a race over a fifty-three mile course, *America* beat every
British boat in both real and corrected time.
While familiar, this story still calls for certain observations.
One reason the Americans sailed to England was to make
money; back then, it would have been inconceivable to race
except for cash wagers – some of them very large. But there
were only a few bets placed against *America* at Cowes,
and Stevens and his partners returned to the United States
having won about $1,000 in wagers, the famous Cup –
an ornate ewer that was made of silver and weighed nearly
eight pounds, and the prize of one hundred guineas that
accompanied the Cup. Before going home, they recovered their
initial outlay by selling *America* to a wealthy Irishman.
The Americans won as a result of superior technology,
among other things. They also won thanks to an interpretation
of the racing instructions that aroused British protest but
was accepted by the race committee.
America passed to the landward side of the Nab lightship,
thus shaving a couple of miles off the course by comparison
with the English yachts, which traditionally sailed outside it.
But she would have won anyway.

Starting with the 1930 challenge, America's Cup
contests were sailed in the legendary boats that
represented the ultimate in yacht racing in the years
between the wars, a time of great advances in sailing's
technologies. Those exceptionally big, technically
sophisticated, spectacular yachts were the bladelike
J-boats with their tall triangles of sail.
The "Js" were designed in accordance
with the Universal Rule perfected by Nat Herreshoff
at the New York Yacht Club's request.
Their deck lengths exceeded thirty-six meters, with
very long overhangs – the length at the waterline was
generally under twenty-six meters – and their sail
plans were extraordinary for the time, very tall in
relation to the base, thus giving the Js a unique,
dramatic appearance in a yachting fleet of schooners
and smaller sloops and cutters.
The Boston designer Frank Paine intended *Yankee*
(seen here) for the 1930 Cup defense, but found his
path barred by that unique concentration of
technology called *Enterprise*, designed by Starling
Burgess. He tried again in 1934, but once again ran up
against a faster competitor: after the very hard-fought
trials, of which *Yankee* won at least ten races, the final
choice fell upon *Rainbow*, another Burgess design.

53

Members of the New York
Yacht Club Race Committee,
1978

54

Loftsman Paul Coble at
Minneford Yacht Yard
circa 1963

Ranger's interior
1937

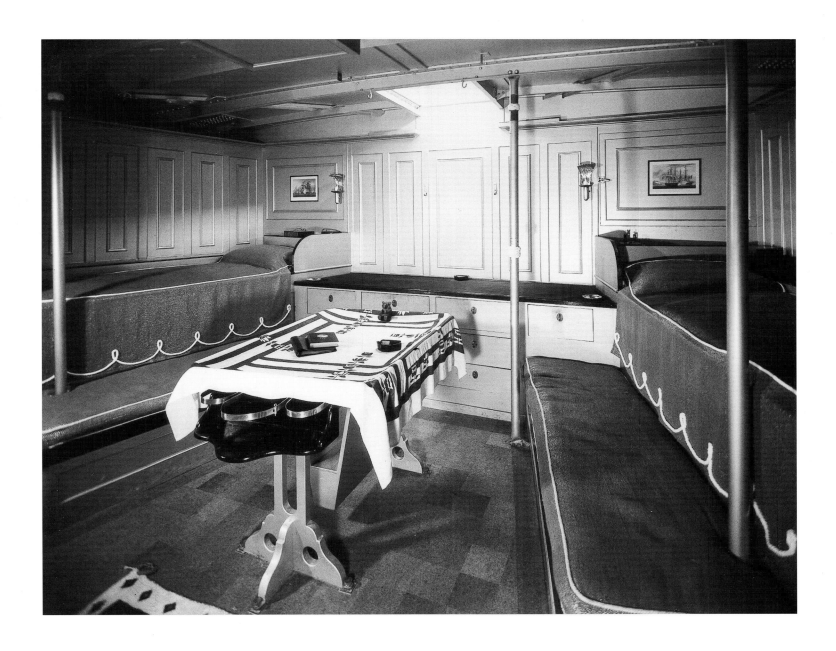

Shamrock V's interior
1930

Sir Thomas J. Lipton
1920

68

Columbia and *Shamrock*
1899

Ranger
1937

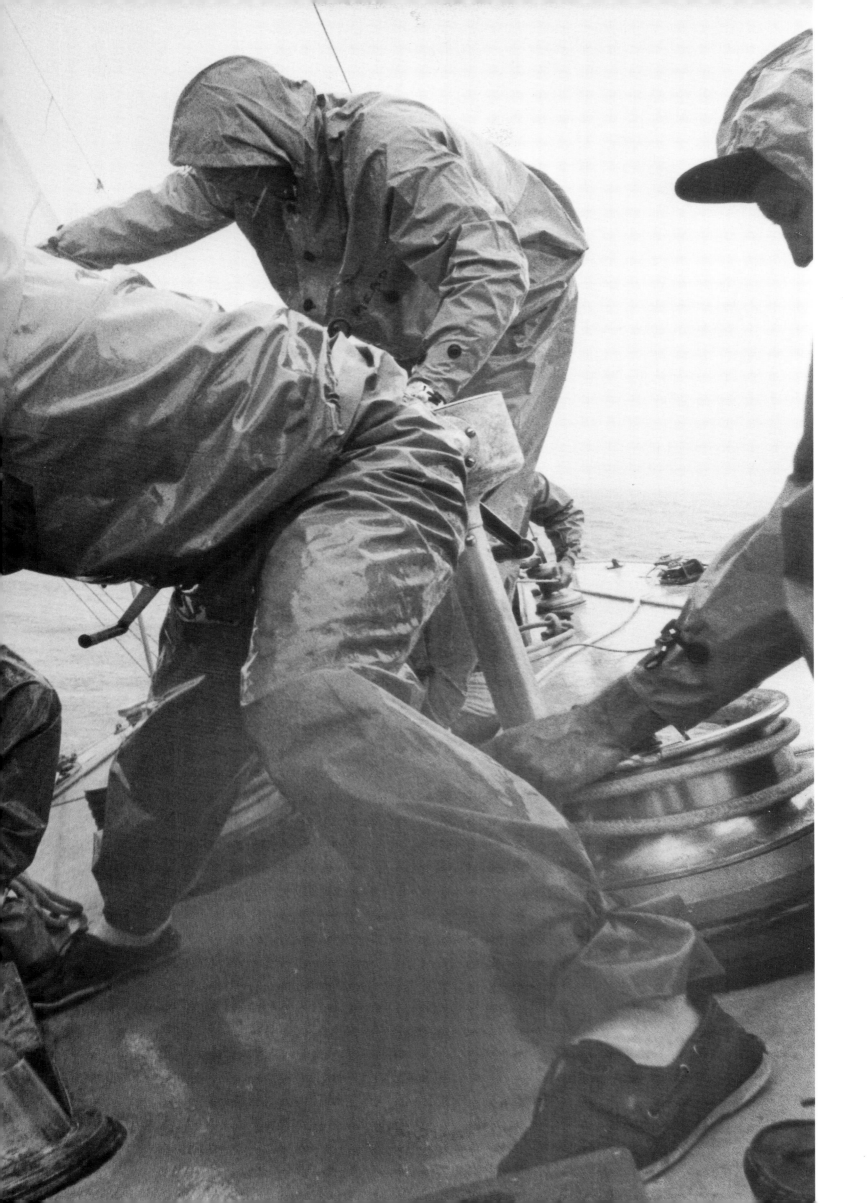

Raimbow
1934

Easterner
1962

77

The New York Yacht Club
Race Committee
1903

78

The New York Yacht Club
America's Cup Committee
1967

79

Endeavour II
1937

Notes on the Plates

1. Hother, 1941

Hother is a typical American cruiser-racer of the 1930s, although a bit atypical, both because she was shaped by the Cox & Stevens design firm, which normally worked on larger power yachts, and because of a canoe stern, an unusual feature in American sailboats, although occasionally found on working boats or on racing yachts such as those designed by L. Francis Herreshoff, son of Captain Nat.

Hother is a good strong cutter of forty-six-feet, built in 1938 by Kretzer Boat Works of City Island, New York. She was built for a Danish-American shipowner, and her canoe stern was modeled after the Danish boats he knew as a boy. *Hother* was successful in ocean racing in the U.S. during the 1930s and 1940s.

2. Mouette, 1933

Twelve-meter International-Rule boats are measured according to the formulas of so-called metric classes which — paralleling the American classes established by Nat Herreshoff's Universal Rule — became active in England starting in 1906, the year the formula came into being. Very large numbers of meter boats were built in the first decades of the century, at first in England and Scotland and in Scandinavia and Germany. Although meter boats became active in the United States only in the twenties, six-meters and twelve-meters were a great success, and in the 1950s the twelves were chosen to compete for the America's Cup.

The twelve-meter yacht was — and, in my opinion, still ought to be — considered a high-performance yacht whether racing or cruising. Those built before the war, like *Mouette*, were also appreciated for their comfortable interiors, which made pleasant day-cruising possible. *Mouette*, which was designed by the great Charles Nicholson, was built in 1928 by Camper & Nicholson at Gosport, England. The photo shows her sailing down Long Island Sound, demonstrating good speed under slackened sail in a light breeze. The stern wave is close to the transom, the wind is at no more than ten knots, and *Mouette* is moving along at about seven knots.

3. Water Gipsy, 1931

Until a few decades ago, ports were only for merchant vessels, and the bays and coves visited by cruising sailors had few docking facilities.

Yachts usually dropped anchor in the roadstead. The need for tenders was therefore much greater than it is today; a good sturdy tender was the anchored yacht's delivery vehicle for guests, water, ice, groceries, anything and everything. North Atlantic fishing schooners — to which the American schooner yacht owes everything — generally carried dories on board, as the steel diesel fishboats that supplanted them still do.

The big schooners that harvested the offshore banks carried as many as 15 dories.

Water Gipsy likewise carries two dories, one nested into the other to take up relatively little space. In inclement weather, the two dories are carried bottom-up at mid-deck.

No more than sixty feet long, this little schooner is extremely elegant: especially the cockpit, with the coaming rounded towards the stern and the two covered companionways, one leading to the owner's cabin and the chartroom, the other to the crew's cabin.

4. Ohyesia, 1894

One of the proofs of yachting's growing popularity and the interest it aroused in the American public is the number of photographers who devoted themselves to documenting its glories, despite the fact that the tools at hand were often unsuited to the task.

Less well-known than the Rosenfelds, Charles Edwin Bolles was among these photographers. This photo, dating from 1894, is more than a century old. It calls for various comments, both technical and social.

Even in the 1890s the "fair sex" was sharing in pleasure boating and other sports. The two ladies on board — who are no exception, as an examination of other photographs in this book will reveal — are taking an active part in sailing this pretty little cutter. While perhaps a bit hampered by their long skirts, they look very *comme il faut* in their sailor's blouses and caps. *Ohyesia* is a small pleasure yacht of a type celebrated in C.P. Kunhardt's *Small Yachts*, published in 1891 — a cruising "cutter," so-called, influenced in America by the cutter yachts of England. Despite the abundant spread of sail, the rigging is designed to be handled by a very small crew: a single reefable jib, a single mainsail that can be handled from the cockpit, no topsails — just a tender in tow and a flag at the masthead. What more do two ladies and two gentlemen need for an idyllic sail?

5. Migrant, 1938

Migrant represents the generation of large yachts that American business tycoons had built for themselves from the last decades of the nineteenth century through the thirties — not just as demonstrations of their wherewithal, but also out of a sincere passion for yachting.

At two hundred and twenty-three feet, she was the longest schooner yacht every built.

Migrant's sturdy rig is descended from the tried-and-true experience of the working schooners that were, from the 1870s into the 1930s, the most commonly employed type of sailing cargo carrier in American coastal waters.

Migrant was launched for Carll Tucker in 1929, the very year the Great Depression began, although desperate economic times did not curtail her sailing, as they did so many others. This impressive black-hulled yacht has had a long life, but has come to an inglorious end. After serving the U.S. Coast Guard in the immediate postwar period, *Migrant* passed into the hands of several new owners and worse circumstances each time. She is still afloat. With a horrible superstructure in place of her now-missing masts, *Migrant* has become a cargo ship in the Caribbean: in short, a banana boat.

6. Coastal cruising, 1934

This photo dates from 1934. Forty years have passed since the picture of *Ohyesia* (plate 4) but except for the rigging and the cut of the clothes not much has changed. The tender in tow and the flag at the masthead are the same as ever. The structure of the yacht does not seem to have changed much, either; above all, the atmosphere of tranquil pleasure on the water is the same.

What has changed is the rigging. Thanks to the appearance of Marconi mainsails, there are no more gaffs calling for involved maneuvering. Everything has become simpler. The triangular sails, not yet so elongated as they were later to become on racing yachts, may look less dashing and elegant than their successors; but they are also more efficient and a great deal easier to handle than their gaff-headed predecessors.

This is a cruising boat, ketch-rigged as so many still are. The mizzen mast makes possible a more horizontal sail plan, and even the bowsprit — never the simplest part of the rigging — can now be shorter.

The yacht has lost something in beauty, but gained in sailing comfort.

A closer look at the cockpit, deckhouse, and even the shape of the portholes reminds us of a style already seen in *Ohyesia*.

Here as there, four people are on board: the ideal number for pleasure sailing.

7. Bow dipping, 1954

Stanley Rosenfeld did not take many pictures from on board. But when he did, he always succeeded in communicating the dynamic qualities of a yacht under sail, as in this 1954 shot. One senses the motion of the water in that slice of wave seen beneath the jib.

There is power in the way the yacht opens a path for itself through the sea. There is tension in that jib full of wind and in the mainsail and boom. Rosenfeld succeeds, as he himself put it, in showing sailing "as it really is." Whether taking pictures of other craft from a position aboard the family photo boat or shooting from on board his subject, he takes you along with him.

Just one criticism: it would be better to turn the wind scoop against the wind. Although Olin and Rod Stephens have already invented the so-called Dorade box, here we still seem resigned to taking on water!

8. Iroquois, 1886

Not too many pleasure boats have been made of steel and not many in the late nineteenth century. Nonetheless, this material was fairly widely used in the United States by the 1880s for commercial vessels and for some yachts.

Photographed at the end of the last century, this schooner is a typical big sailing yacht of the 1880s and 1890s. *Iroquois* employs shapes and solutions standard in its period such as the clipper bow and the centerboard perfected in response to a need for yachts and commercial vessels of all sizes to sail in the shallow waters of many American harbors and waterways.

In March of 1888, *Iroquois* survived a sudden, unexpected storm along the American coastline, a storm in which a sistership went down with all hands.

These very years saw the beginnings of sharp debate about the design of both fishing schooners and schooner yachts: hulls of shallow draft whose stability under sail depended largely upon their width and their centerboards. Design was soon to evolve in the direction of hulls of deeper draft and with a fixed keel rather than a centerboard.

The dangerous bowsprit would also disappear in the new century. *Iroquois* was designed in 1886 by A. Cary Smith, a collaborator of Robert Center's who had important responsibilities at the New York Yacht Club as an organizer of the trials for the selection of America's Cup defenders.

9. Brown Smith Jones, 1935

At the end of the nineteenth century, in the shallow waters of Chesapeake Bay – that huge bay that extends more than a hundred and fifty miles from Virginia north into Maryland, there developed a type of boat equipped for oyster fishing, an evolution of the Chesapeake Bay log canoe. This picturesque workboat, with the equally charming name of "bugeye," was often used for recreational sailing, either newly built as a yacht or converted from oyster boat to pleasure boat.

As with many American working vessels, the rigging is very simple, thus allowing for a small crew. The jib has a short spar at its base that makes it self-tacking; there are no topsails; and the masts are sturdy and raked aft, Chesapeake-style. While the mainsail and mizzen in this 1935 photo are of the Marconi type, the proportion of base to height is so emphatically inelegant as to have given this type of sail the nickname "leg of mutton." The triangular leg-of-mutton sails of these and other Virginia and Maryland workboats actually precede the similar Bermudian or Marconi sails of twentieth-century yachts.

The whole thing may not be very efficient from an aerodynamic standpoint; but this crew of three appears to be sailing along with no trouble at all.

10. Sea Cloud, 1939

In 1931 the Krupp shipyard of Kiel in Germany built one of the last "floating palaces," as a journalist of the time called the yachts of over two hundred feet so much in vogue in the United States between 1920 and 1930. The vessel's original name was *Hussar*, changed to *Sea Cloud* in 1936, and the overall length of this four-master was more than a hundred meters. The owner was a woman believed at that time to be the richest in the world, and certainly the richest in the United States: Marjorie Merriweather Post, rich in her own right, and married to financier E.F. Hutton.

Hussar/Sea Cloud was designed by Cox & Stevens, specialists in the design of large luxury yachts. For such projects, steel was the proper choice, and German shipyards had long experience with this material.

This ship-sized yacht was very luxuriously furnished and finished, with marble floors in the bathrooms, deep carpeting in the saloons, and antique furniture and crystal chandeliers in the cabins. She remained the property of Marjorie Post even after her divorce from E.F. Hutton and her marriage to the American diplomat Joseph E. Davies. And she remained active, taking Mr. and Mrs. Davies to Leningrad in 1936 when Joe Davies became Ambassador to Russia, and remaining until 1938 as a floating residence and an example to the Soviets of capitalist decadence. After service with the U.S. Coast Guard during the war she remained Marjorie Post's yacht until 1955 when she was sold to Rafael Trujillo, dictator of the Dominican Republic. *Sea Cloud* had several other owners after Trujillo, finally being bought by German businessmen who gave her a seven-million-dollar refit at the beginning of the 1980s. *Sea Cloud* now sails as a luxury charter ship.

11. Istalena, 1930

Francis Herreshoff believed in the canoe stern, a structural solution dear to such designers as the Argentinian Manuel Campos and – here we're really at the antipodes – the Norwegian Colin Archer.

Captain Nat's son offered double ends on *Whirlwind*, the beautiful J-Class contender he designed for the 1930 trials to choose the defender of the America's Cup. *Whirlwind* never got close; out of twenty-five trial races she won just one.

Istalena was built in the designer's family shipyard, the Herreshoff Manufacturing Company of Bristol, Rhode Island. She measured eighty-seven feet overall and fifty-four at the waterline, qualifying for the M-Class under the Universal Rule developed at the beginning of the century by Nat Herreshoff himself.

We know about two predecessors of *Istalena*: an eighty-five foot K-Class from 1907, and a New York Yacht Club fifty-footer, both designed for the same owner by the great Nat. This *Istalena* was very successful in M-Class racing in the early 1930s.

In this photo, *Istalena* is rather out of trim: the large jib is making the boat heel far over, while the mainsail is stalling.

The sailors on the lee side appear to be the only ones interested in the yacht's progress, with most of the people in the cockpit paying attention to the photographer instead.

12. Anchorite, 1950

The photo dates from 1950, but this beautiful fifty-foot yawl was built back in 1934, to a design by Owen Merrill. The builder, Nevins of City Island, New York, was perhaps the most skillful builder of yachts in the United States from the 1920s until the end of the 1950s.

The rigging is typical of the late thirties, a yawl rig favored by the Cruising Club of America rating rule for ocean racing, and here missing the large Genoa jib common on yachts like this in the 1950s. The widespread adoption of the Genoa was determined by technical considerations: less elastic synthetic fabrics, a narrower base for the shrouds, allowing coverage of the Genoa, more powerful winches.

Anchorite is working hard, sailing close to the wind and driving into a choppy sea. It's a fine day. The sky shows that there's a wind up; and the sailors, seemingly expecting a few more knots of it, are already reefing the mainsail and the small yankee. On a brisk day like this, it's best to think ahead!

13. Valkyrie, 1946

Things look to have gotten a bit out of hand here. Water is coming into the cockpit, and the jib is holding several gallons, too. But the crew doesn't seem unduly bothered. Either they are well acquainted with their yacht's limitations, or else they haven't a clue what to do.

The helmsman appears to be getting ready to luff; the crew member manning the jib sheet is looking at something up forward; another sailor is hanging onto the cockpit coaming; and the fourth is taking shelter. They ought to be paying out the mainsheet, closing the companionway, and hurrying to take in sail!

Of course, it's easy to criticize when you're sitting in a comfortable armchair. What's probably happened is that a sudden gust has caught the crew by surprise when the boat wasn't going very fast. In such a situation, the wind's sudden power only makes a boat heel over.

Valkyrie is a fine design executed shortly after the war for Stuart Kay by Phil Rhodes, who was very prolific over a long career. Born in 1895, Rhodes designed his first boat in 1919. In the fifties he was still capable of designing the Fastnet winner *Carina*, and he designed successful yachts into the sixties.

14. Saraband 1936

Saraband was designed by Nat Herreshoff in 1906. At the new century's start, the great designer had moved on from cutters and yawls to schooners, inaugurating a splendid period of work on such vessels with *Ingomar* in 1903.

The boat in the photo is a typical American schooner yacht of the Edwardian era.

Compared to the English schooner, the rigging is a bit simpler, with just two headsails at the bow and no gaffs on the topsails. The design of the deckhouse is also very American. It's low and boxy, with windows on three sides; Herreshoff was to repeat it in many other designs. This large yacht of ninety-one feet – owned in the 1930s by John Nicholas Brown, the gentleman in a blazer, tie, and cap behind the helmsman – is sailing close-hauled in a stiff breeze. It's a stupendous day to be out on the water, and the high bulwark is keeping the cockpit nice and dry. The three lifebuoys at the stern are typical of American yachts, and they're a good idea.

15. Avatar, 1968

The sixties represented a period of transition between custom-built classic yachts and modern fiberglass boats built in multiples.

Avatar still honors wood's historical contribution to sailing with her sweep of laid-teak deck, mahogany cockpit coaming, and a lazarette hatch where only the plexiglass, even if studded with screws, announces "modern."

Even in her deckhouse, which is unmistakably made of fiberglass, the designer has paid tribute to the old ways with a little frame of wood, almost as though he were embarrassed by the sleek new material.

With a deck length of nearly sixteen meters, this boat was built in 1965 by the Dutch shipyard LeComte to a design by William Tripp.

The only person on board who seems interested in making the yacht go faster is the helmsman; but this is as it should be. When you're out sailing, the deck should not be seen only as a place to pull ropes and grind winches. The sky, the sea, and the company on board are the real reason to be there!

16. Rita Irene, 1936

When wind and tide are at loggerheads, especially in shallow water, the waves get very short and steep; such conditions are hard on any yacht. The little schooner in the photo, *Rita Irene*, is shown sailing against the current in the Sound near Lloyd Harbor, Long Island, in the Spring of '36.

Here the bow has suddenly shot up, trying to break through the wave, which has shattered under the impact, drenching the deck and, naturally, the people in the cockpit. The next step will be for the bowsprit to dive sharply downwards, with the bow smashing the sea and the yacht losing its headway. So matters will get even worse when the next wave arrives a few seconds later.

Not even the most fanatical sailor enjoys *this* sort of wet, wild progress!

17. Square-rigger deck, 1929

From the standpoint of naval architecture, the windjammers brought many innovations: the central quarterdeck, for example, which sheltered the helmsman, who had previously been all the way aft, from great waves breaking over the stern; or the enclosed wheelhouse; or what was called in these vessels a flying bridge, a raised catwalk that allowed sailors to reach safely the areas where they needed to be even when the deck was awash. In this photo, the central quarterdeck is clearly visible; and it is easy to see how this structure offered more safety than a steering station aft.

The masts support an impressive amount of rigging. The cables are made of steel, a much stronger material than the traditional hemp and sisal, and this helps the masts – themselves now made of steel – to withstand greater pressures of wind and gyration.

In comparison to the softer reactions of the wood and cloth of deepwater vessels that came before the big metal windjammers, steel produced new sounds, and these may be sensed in the picture. The shrouds emit audible vibrations; the blocks give off an infernal clangor as they smack against the steel spars; the scupper hatches, also made of steel, clank as they open and close; and there is a constant soft groaning as background from the riveted steel plating!

18. Square-rigger deck, 1929

On board these large sailing vessels, as on the earlier clippers, the crew was kept ceaselessly busy. Aside from the business of sailing, there were equally demanding jobs of maintenance and repair. (While sailing in the Indian Ocean, it fell to the crew of *Cutty Sark* to replace the rudder using materials available on board: a blow from the sea had ripped out both the wooden blade and its iron armature.) Sailors were also responsible for order and cleanliness on board. Tradition demanded that everything be "ship-shape" when the vessel sailed into port – especially its home port, where it would be subject to the scrutiny of its owner.

During months at sea, the planking of the deck had borne the harsh effects of saltwater and of the constant caulking of the seams, an operation carried out before and after each storm to keep the deck watertight. Here we see the deck and other structures being given a thorough cleaning with mops, holy stones, and lots of water. After cleaning, some captains liked to have a mixture of oil and citron applied to the planking, in order to make the wood brighter and shinier.

19. Tusitala, 1929

The hardest task of all aboard a sailing ship was shortening sail in a storm, the crew climbing onto the yards when they were wet, the canvas soaked and cold-hardened, and the footropes sometimes slippery with ice. They might have to make this climb at night, with the ship rolling violently in the wind and lashed with rain!

The big sailing ships started to take in sail with the wind over forty knots, dousing the high sails first: royals, skysail, and high staysails. Above fifty knots, it was time to strike the main course, the flying jibs, and the upper topgallants. When the wind rose past sixty, it was the turn of the lower topgallants, the fore staysail and other low staysails, and the spanker. At seventy knots, it was time to strike the jib and the lower topsails.

Tusitala is carrying no sail on its mizzenmast. On the mainmast, the main lower topsail has blown out before the crew managed to get it furled, and only the main upper topsail is still up. In these wild conditions, one wonders where the photographer can have been: probably high on the foremast and thus, one presumes, around forty meters above the deck – with bulky equipment to carry and use successfully!

20. Cutty Sark, 1922

The caption accompanying this photo tells us that the ship bears the same name as the famous clipper *Cutty Sark*. But it is no insult to this typical American cargo schooner to say that its more celebrated British namesake (whose name, taken from a poem by Robert Burns, means "short shirt") had far nobler lines. The original *Cutty Sark* was a clipper used first on the tea run and later for carrying grain. It sailed the long sea lanes linking China and Australia with England, in unceasing competition with its peers, before finally tying up in glory at London's National Maritime Museum.

The type of multi-masted schooner shown here carried bulk cargo up and down the North American coastline from the beginning of the twentieth century into the 1930s. The low cost at which such vessels could be built and operated made them viable competitors of steamships. This four-masted schooner usually carried a cargo of wood.

Thanks to its schooner rig of many relatively small sails, few of them requiring men to go aloft, a small crew was able to work the ship with relative ease in the shifting coastal winds.

Another Rosenfeld photo, dating from the late twenties, shows six vessels of this type waiting for the tide to change before sailing out Long Island Sound for points North. These ships often looked run-down, with peeling paint on the hulls and patched sails, as is the case with our *Cutty Sark*; but this in no way diminishes their charm.

21. Tusitala, 1925

In 1925, forty-two years after her launching, the full-rigged ship *Tusitala* was still carrying cargo from the coasts of Africa to New York for the Farrell Lines. The ship had no engine power. In the photo, the wind is apparently too light to swell the canvas sails, which could weigh as much as a ton when dry, and more than that when rain or sea spray had soaked them through.

It was a good thing that the windjammers were equipped with steam winches for working the sails and yards, since this made it possible for such large-capacity vessels to operate very efficiently and with a relatively small crew. For example, the full-rigged ship *Preussen*, considered the largest of all the German, English, and Finnish windjammers, built in the Tecklenborg shipyards in Germany in 1902, had an overall length of one hundred thirty-three meters and carried eight thousand tons of cargo with a crew of just forty-five men.

Thirty years earlier the clipper ship *Cutty Sark*, with thirty-five men on board, was able to load only one thousand three hundred tons of cargo. Carrying bulk cargoes such as coal, grain and guano with such capacity and efficiency permitted the big iron and steel windjammers to operate profitably well into the twentieth century.

22. Seven Seas, 1935

The windjammers were sailing ships designed to go around Cape Horn: a route difficult for steamships on account of the length of the passage and the absence of places where they could refuel.

The big, boxy windjammers often carried two types of cargo made dangerous by their inflammability: coal and nitrates, for which the rapid growth of industrialization and rising requirements for foodstuffs had created an ever-increasing demand.

Much bigger than the celebrated clippers, these ships generally had a deck length of around a hundred meters, as against the sixty or seventy meters of their predecessors. They carried more sail, were more powerful, and could transport far greater loads; at the same time, they were just as fast as the clippers and required fewer crew.

This last blaze of sailing-ship glory was made possible by steel, which was used in every part of these ships, especially for masts and rigging. They were the last of the great sailing ships, and they were busy and profitable in the first three decades of the twentieth century. A photo taken in the Australian port of Newcastle in 1900 shows as many as fifteen windjammers waiting to take on coal bound for Chile, where the ships would load new cargoes of nitrates in the form of guano. *Seven Seas* was built in Sweden in 1912.

23. Fishing schooner, 1922

If the greatest challenge for the big sailing ships was going around Cape Horn, winter on the North Atlantic fishing banks represented an equally demanding test for American fishing schooners. At those latitudes, around 45° N, snowstorms were frequent, and weather was made volatile by the meeting of the cold Labrador Current and the warmer Gulf Stream. During the rare breaks in the bad weather, the crew struggled to clear the deck. Five inches of snow meant an extra load of several tons carried above the waterline, making the boat dangerously top-heavy.

Freezing rain or mist that covered decks, deckhouses, spars and rigging with ice was even more dangerous and more difficult than snow to remove.

The North American fishing fleet lost great numbers of vessels and human lives during the last half of the nineteenth century: the annual average was twenty schooners and one hundred fifty-three deaths.

Above and beyond the weather, this tragic situation was also a result of the design of fishing hulls – shapes determined by the demands of work, the desire to sail fast to market with a load of fish, and the need to operate in shallow waters.

The end of the nineteenth century saw efforts to develop safer hulls with deep keels instead of centerboards, shorter rigs, blunter bows with shorter bowsprits, and finally no bowsprits at all – eliminating the "widow-makers" that had killed so many men who fell off them while wrestling with headsails.

24. Crew on a square-rigger, 1929

Only towards the end of the nineteenth century, after 1880, did winches make their appearance aboard large sailing vessels as an aid to managing sails, spars, and running rigging. Their inventor – or more precisely, the man who devised their application – was a skilled and experienced Scottish skipper named J.C.B. Jarvis. Winches were used to hoist sails, to maneuver the yards, and to haul the braces taut; other tasks involved in sail-handling and trimming continued to be done with human muscle and sheer numbers, as we see here.

25. Henry Ford, 1923

Henry Ford was one of the New England fishing schooners that raced
in Massachusetts Bay in 1923 for the honor of facing a Canadian schooner
in the third series of the International Fishermen's Cup Races.
That year the new schooner *Columbia* was chosen to challenge for the Cup
that had been won by the new Canadian schooner *Bluenose* in 1921.
The unbeatable *Bluenose* defended successfully, as she would for the next
fifteen years of these amazing races.
Here we see *Henry Ford* with six feet of water burying her lee rail while
the crew stands calmly up to windward. Even though this powerful
schooner was not chosen to sail to Halifax and try to regain
the Fishermen's Cup, we can see that she was being sailed to the limit
in the trials.

26. Robt. Jno. Beswick, 1924

This is a photo not only of a schooner but a way of life.
The eighty-foot coasting schooner *Robt. Jno. Beswick* was built in 1901,
and in 1924 was carrying cargo to and from the Long Island Sound port
of New Haven. Small schooners like her, sometimes owned by families,
carried cargo up and down the U.S. East Coast from the middle
of the nineteenth century into the nineteen-thirties — wood, coal, building
materials, manufactured goods, farm produce.
Without an engine, the *Beswick* is being pushed here by her gasoline-
powered yawl boat lashed astern. The family sits on deck and watches
the photographer. This little schooner looks very shipshape
and fresh-painted, perhaps appropriate for a vessel kept proudly
by a family — a vessel that is not only their livelihood but their home.

27. Splicing rope, 1938

Perhaps a hundred separate tasks needed to be carried out to maintain
the efficiency of a ship and its rigging, and they were all indispensable in
using the wind to best advantage and ensuring a safe return to port.
Splicing lines, sheets, halyards, stoppers and so forth was one such task.
The marlinspike is an extension of the sailor's fingers, helping him exploit
his strength and skill. Rudimentary as it is, this tool makes possible
the sophisticated and even artistic skills of a sailor's ropework — what the
sailors proudly call "marlinspike seamanship."
The Rosenfelds' pictures seem intent upon communicating a large vision
of the world of sailing and the sea: a vision more focused upon man's
relationship to maritime activity than that of the Beken family, who may
be regarded as the Rosenfelds' English counterparts among yachting
photographers. While the Bekens emphasized sailing's spectacular aspects,
the power and beauty of the vessels themselves, their seaworthiness and
ability to stand up to the wind, the Rosenfelds were always conscious
of human action.
Here the focus of the image is the activity itself, just as the sailor's mind
must have been focused when he concentrated on controlling the strands
of rope — following and exploiting the material's natural curves instead
of fighting them.

28-29. Kaiser's Cup Race, 1905

This picture is by James Burton, another American photographer who —
along with J.C. Hemment, J.S. Johnston, C.E. Bolles, and N.C. Stebbins —
recorded a great period in the history of yachting: a greatness confirmed
by the close attention the press and the public of the time devoted
to the subject.
We are at Sandy Hook, New Jersey, the real entrance to New York harbor,
witnessing the start of the 1905 Kaiser's Cup, a race across an ocean
promoted by the German monarch, himself an enthusiastic yachtsman
and owner of racing yachts named *Meteor*. Competitors were to sail three
thousand nautical miles to Lizard Head on the southwestern coast
of England.
The officials, on board the lightship *Sandy Hook*, have fired the cannon
shot signaling the race's beginning: the puff of white smoke hides
the schooner at the extreme right. The first two competitors
(the three-masted schooner hidden by the smoke and the big brig)
are sheering off so as to avoid a false start.
Among the participants, a total of eleven yachts, are: *Fleur de Lys*,
a thirty-three-meter American schooner; the seventy-four-meter English
brig *Valhalla*; *Endymion*, another American schooner of forty-five meters;
Ailsa, a thirty-eight-meter yawl; *Hildegarde*, yet another American
schooner of forty-one meters; and *Hamburg*, the only German vessel
in the race. The last entry is *Atlantic*, the three-masted schooner destined
to win this long, hard test, setting a record by crossing to England
in twelve days and four hours. This record would stand
for more than 90 years.

30. N.Y.Y.C. Cruise, 1955

One may count as many as thirty-two sailboats in this picture.
There are undoubtedly others outside the frame to the right (a bit too far
to windward with respect to the buoy), along with more even farther off.
So there's not much elbow room in this 1955 version of the New York
Yacht Club Cruise, the fleet filling their sails on an easy sea.
A bit of current may be detected under the buoy, pushing the boats to
leeward. The yacht leading the group has raised the head of the swinging
boom so as to open out the spinnaker a little and catch a bit more wind;
but this might also increase the leeway. It's a tough calculation.
Meanwhile, the boats to windward have borne up at the buoy,
while those to leeward have already slackened their spinnakers, hardening
up on the wind with the Genoa.
It's a typical end-of-regatta scene. The sun is setting and the wind has died
down, but the finish line is near and the sea is calm. The boats, at least
those in the foreground, are maintaining a certain speed, and their sails
are still billowing. There's not much more you can ask of a regatta –
except, of course, to win it.

31. Larchmont Yacht Club One-Designs, 1924

Rules governing the classes and the course have always been indispensable
aspects of yacht racing. And so have yacht clubs. In Great Britain – which
led the way with the first yacht club, the Water Club of the Harbour
of Cork, founded as early as 1720 – such clubs have always had (as they still
have) a snobbish exclusiveness. In the United States, on the other hand,
the entrance ticket was most often sheer wealth. The founders
and members could not be drawn from the nobility, since the country
didn't have one. Instead, they were industrial tycoons, publishers,
and bankers: in short, the rising rulers of the world.
By the end of the nineteenth century, North America had more than eighty
yacht clubs, with the deep and sheltered waters of New York's Long Island
Sound home to as many as twenty of them. Of these, the most famous was,
and is, the New York Yacht Club, founded in 1844 by John Cox Stevens and
eight of his friends. Another eminent club is the Larchmont Yacht Club. In
the twenties, it was the setting for great sailing challenges:
the "one-designs" in the photo were, in a sense, this club's answer
to the New York Yacht Club's thirty-footers and fifty-footers.
Larchmont Race Week is still one of the largest one-design racing events
in the world.

32. Atlantic, 1933

The great three-masted schooner *Atlantic* was designed in 1903 by William
Gardner of New York, later to create both *Vanitie*, a yacht intended
to be defender of the America's Cup in 1914, and a little single-stick racer
destined to be the most competitive and long-lived one-design of all:
the Starboat.
Launched in 1904, *Atlantic* was entered by her owner Wilson Marshall
in a U.S.-to-England race called the Kaiser's Cup for its benefactor,
the German monarch. At the helm of his fifty-six-meter schooner,
Marshall placed a famous Scottish skipper who had already defended
the America's Cup three times – Charlie Barr. The incomparable Captain
Barr lived up to his reputation. *Atlantic* won, setting a new speed record
for the crossing into the bargain. After that triumph, *Atlantic* continued
an illustrious career. She crossed the ocean for which she was named once
again in 1928, sailing that year's trans-Atlantic race to Spain,
and hosted many famous figures, including King George V of England,
a great sailing enthusiast.

33. Commodore Nichols, Seawanhaka Corinthian Yacht Club, 1921

Boats have certainly changed, so have regattas, and so has the clothing
people wear to go sailing. Today no one would dream of showing up
on the water dressed like George Nichols, Vice Commodore
of the Seawanhaka Corinthian Yacht Club, here seen in 1921 relaxing
at the companionway of his six-meter during a race in Oyster Bay.
But the most striking thing is the naturalness with which Commodore
Nichols – like Charles Francis Adams, or like Mike Vanderbilt,
with his professional and amateur crew members, or like many others
of that era in white shirt and necktie – goes out for a sail.
In 1921 there was none of that paraphernalia of specialized yachting
clothes, ultra-waterproof slickers, and high-tech footgear that we now
regard as indispensable!

34. Chesapeake sailing canoe, 1929

The big yachts competed in the ocean, but on the sheltered bays
of the United States there developed such extraordinary boats as
the sandbagger (which owed its capacity for carrying so much sail to
its wide hull, and to the bags of sand shifted by the crew from one side to
the other), or this canoe, which stays on its feet thanks to the weight
of the men sitting outboard at the ends of long planks.
Tacks could be executed with no need to touch the sheets.
As the bow turned into the wind, the sailors pulled in the long planks,
ready to push them outboard on the other side as needed.
This was the only sail-handling required of the seven crew members.
The shroudless masts did not permit a vertical sail plan; there was,
accordingly, an effort to achieve the greatest possible horizontal sail area,
leading to an unusual system of spars to stiffen the rig. Something similar
is still to be seen in certain parts of the Caribbean.

35. Elizabeth Ann Howard, 1923

As the sun sets, two fishing schooners sail back to Gloucester after a day
of racing on Massachusetts Bay. The photographer, Morris Rosenfeld,
is aboard the schooner *Henry Ford*—here under calmer conditions than
those he experienced when he took the photograph numbered twenty-five
in these pages! The other schooner is *Elizabeth Ann Howard*, and this
photo lets us appreciate how yacht-like the North Atlantic fishing
schooners were. Neither the *Ford* nor the *Howard* were chosen to uphold
the honor of Gloucester in the 1923 series of International Fishermen's
Cup Races sailed at Halifax, Nova Scotia.

36. At the Start, 1930

A gaff-rigged cutter, more a cruiser than a racer, a lean Marconi-rigged
sloop hard on the wind, and several other boats, large and small,
maneuver at the start of one of the races of Larchmont Race Week in 1930.
This one is a Handicap-Class race, involving a mixed group of yachts,
and in the brisk wind we see here it will be an interesting thing to watch.
Like Cowes Week in England and Kiel Week in Germany, Larchmont
Race Week was (as it still is) a big and exciting race meeting for boats
of many sizes and classes.

37. International knockdown, 1941

The crews of International One-Designs always took their boats
to the limit, engaging in hair-raising tacking duels. These boats were built
just for racing, and offered helmsmen and crews an agile, high-strung
sailing machine with capabilities comparable to those of the Dragon,
the six-meter, or the modern Soling, to mention a few international sailing
classes with similar characteristics.
In this 1941 photo, wind conditions look pretty extreme for flying
a spinnaker. In such a situation, the helmsman needs all his sensitivity
to feel a yaw coming, and bear up just enough to avoid it.
But not a bit more, since this is a race and there's no time to lose!
Here the trailing boat has taken a knockdown and both mainsail
and spinnaker have hit the water. The only thing to be done now is to get
the spinnaker in. When the boat straightens up, the crew will square away
the spinnaker and start afresh.
But the rival boat to windward must have picked up a good fifty meters
in the meantime, and in these wind conditions it will be hard to win back.
Unless the rival, too, has a similar mishap...

38. J-Boats, 1937

This photo shows the end of an era: five of the great J-Boats sailing
in the 1937 New York Yacht Club Cruise. *Endeavour I*, sail number K4,
and *Endeavour II*, K6, T.O.M. Sopwith's two Camper & Nicholson boats,
are off to a very good start, just ahead of the Americans. Of the latter,
Rainbow — the farthest to windward — was designed by Starling Burgess
and had previously defeated *Endeavour I* to defend the America's Cup
in 1934; *Ranger*, sail number J5, is a newcomer born of a design
collaboration by Burgess and Olin Stephens for Harold Vanderbilt,
and destined to defend the Cup in 1937 by defeating *Endeavour II*;
finally there is the old *Yankee*, designed by Frank Paine, a powerful boat
that came close to being chosen to defend the Cup in 1930 and 1934.
The only one of these five noble boats still sailing is the first *Endeavour*,
restored in the 1980s by the American yachtswoman Elizabeth Meyer.

39. International One-Designs, 1941

As Cowes saw the beginnings and success of the Beken family of yacht
photographers, Long Island Sound saw the origins and development
of the Rosenfelds' huge body of work.
Our photographers would position themselves near a buoy and wait,
and have their wait rewarded by such subjects as the dramatic dance
of these three International One-Designs. The positioning and the waiting
were easy; the great thing — the skillful and artistic thing — was to release
the camera's shutter just at a moment like this. Stanley Rosenfeld makes
it seem simple: "In 1930 it was just a question of waiting for a sudden
change in the weather to provide some moments of dramatic action."
In this photo, three International One-Designs — a class popular
on Long Island Sound, in Bermuda, and in Scandinavia — are engaged
in a tacking duel as they come up to the buoy. The helmsman
in the foreground has very properly borne up at the last moment,
and is watching the stern of number 7 as it sails by.
Number 22 is going by quietly. It has done the intelligent thing in bearing
up earlier: now number 7, being covered, can no longer do so — while
number 22 is in too favorable a position to want to do so!

40. New York Yacht Club 70-footers, 1900

The largest class of U.S. one designs, the New York Yacht Club 70-footers
were designed and built by Nathanael Herreshoff in 1900.
Four of these big sloops with long ends, towering sailplans,
and too-delicate construction were built, and here we see them
racing in a good breeze. They were not successful.
Their scowline wooden hulls were unable to take the strains
of racing, and they worked and leaked so much that
they acquired the nickname "leakabouts."
Nevertheless, they are full of grace and power as we see them here

41. Stormy Weather, 1937

In 1930 the young American designer Olin Stephens created
a revolutionary fifty-two-foot yacht that presaged most of the structural
features of the cruising-racing boats of the following forty years.
His *Dorade* won a trans-Atlantic race in 1931, then won the 1931 Fastnet
Race and repeated this Fastnet victory in 1933. In 1934, the same designer
was to create a formidable descendent of *Dorade* in *Stormy Weather*.
Beamier than her predecessor, *Stormy Weather* had an enviable record.
In 1935 she won another trans-Atlantic race and then the Fastnet;
the following year she won her class in the Bermuda Race.
Yawl-rigged like *Dorade*, *Stormy* has a mizzen so very far aft as to require
an outrigger for the sheet. She can sail very close to the wind,
a characteristic of all Olin Stephens designs. In this 1937 photo, *Stormy
Weather* is seen sailing close-hauled in a stiff wind through turbulent
waters on her way to the Gulf Stream: the dark strip straight ahead
of the bow.

42. Star class, 1950

The position of this helmsman and crewman is such a classic, and so unique to this boat, that, even if the boat were airbrushed out of the photo, any sailor could tell you: it's a Star!

This lively one-design was a product of William Gardner's New York design office, and from the day the first boat was launched in1911 the Star has been the star performer among the small racing classes. Gardner was a most versatile designer, responsible for the 1914 *Vanitie*, intended for the America's Cup, as well as that largest and most beautiful of all yachts, the fifty-six meter *Atlantic*. Today the Starboat races all over the world, and for nearly ninety years it has been the best training ground for racing helmsmen. As for the Star's crewman, as we see here, all he needs to be is heavy!

43. Dyna, 1962

Dyna is a fifty-eight foot ketch built in 1957 by the Burger Boat Company of Manitowoc, Wisconsin, on the shore of Lake Michigan, a builder whose history goes back to 1863 with wooden shipbuilding and, in this century, yachtbuilding.

Sparkman & Stephens, the world-famous design firm that Olin Stephens had opened in partnership with his brother Rod and the yacht broker Drake Sparkman in 1929, designed *Dyna* for construction in marine aluminum, a material that had advantages of light weight and extreme stiffness for racing yachts like this one.

In the photo, *Dyna* is running before a brisk afternoon southwesterly off Newport, Rhode Island. Her sails are well set and well tended – in fact, the good-sized, perfectly trimmed spinnaker has her practically skimming the water.

44. Hinckley Pilot, 1949

It used to be said (and it's still true today) that there are three basic requirements in boat design – speed, safety, and comfort, and that all three cannot be met simultaneously. Each must always be sacrificed to some degree to the others, with the choice depending on local conditions, the type of sailing foreseen, the owner's sailing philosophy, and perhaps many less obvious factors. This was why one boat rarely resembled another in the custom-building era before World War II, and these differences constituted, at least in part, each boat's fascination.

Following the Second World War, there appeared standardized, series-produced, all-the-same models of boats in greater numbers than ever before. Henry Hinckley and his boatyard in Maine made their reputation in postwar America building a fleet of such stock boats. The company is still building boats today, and is distinguished in the now-international yacht market by boats of classic design in which wood plays an important part.

Here we're already in the modern era. The boat in this 1949 photo displays the loss of personality we've been talking about. She's the wooden ancestor of the countless fiberglass stock boats that began to come along in the 1950s.

45. Lutine, 1952

This 1952 photo shows the pure essence of offshore racing – a pursuit that combines competition (and with it the capacity to exploit the forces of nature by means of technique and technology) and navigation (successfully finding the way from one place to another, a part of sailing since its beginnings).

In this picture, *Lutine* seems at one with everything around her: the sails with the clouds, the hull with the boundless sea. The men on board also look to be in perfect harmony with the whole. *Lutine* was built by Camper & Nicholson in England, to a design by Laurent Giles the same year the picture was taken. At that time, as often in its history, offshore yacht racing was split between the American rating rules developed by the Cruising Club of America, and the European rules developed by England's Royal Ocean Racing Club. Giles designed *Lutine* with an eye on both sets of rules, creating a competitor with a good rating under both systems. *Lutine* turned out to be an excellent racer, especially in Europe, where she twice won the Fastnet, in 1953 and 1955.

46. Seascape, 1938

The waters of the U.S. East Coast have long offered ideal conditions
for yachting at its best, from one-design racing in sheltered water to
cruising and racing in the ocean. Protected, shallow waters are common:
New York's Long Island Sound, Massachusetts Bay, Nantucket Sound
and Vineyard Sound, Buzzard's Bay, Chesapeake Bay. These are all places
where, safe from ocean waves, yachts large and small meet the challenges
of contrary currents and capricious winds.
Weather conditions here change often and abruptly, especially along
the coast of New England. At these latitudes, depressions form along
the unstable front between Arctic cold moving across the continent
and tropical warmth coming in from the sea. Winds of different speeds,
blowing in opposite directions, cause a clash and churning of air masses.
Matters are further complicated along shore by the influence of the great
currents: the cold Labrador Current that can meander down the coastline
as far south as the latitude of Baltimore; and the warm Gulf Stream
which, arriving from the southwest, changes direction where it meets the
other current. Some of this meteorological flux can be seen in the photo.
The low cumulus clouds and thunderclouds threaten gusting winds
and some violent cloudbursts, although all is still serene on this sea dotted
with sailboats.

47. Ingomar and Elmina, ca. 1908

From the time of the schooner yacht *America* in the middle
of the nineteenth century and up until the thirties, schooners found favor
with racing yachtsmen in the United States.
In 1903, Nat Herreshoff planned the steel schooner *Ingomar*, the first
of a long series of boats of this type, for the financier Morton F. Plant.
Elmina, leading *Ingomar* here, was designed by A. Cary Smith and built
in steel by Townsend & Downey for Frederick Brewster.
The photo is by James Burton, one of the early yacht photographers whose
work was acquired by Morris Rosenfeld. *Elmina* has a lead on *Ingomar*,
but does not have all her sails properly trimmed; both yachts must have
tacked just now. (The man on the spreader must furl the gaff-topsail each
time, so that it may be moved to the other side.) Aboard *Ingomar*,
they have already hoisted the flying jib. *Elmina* has not yet done so,
and the foresail sheet has not yet been hauled taut.

48. Water Gipsy, 1936

The schooners *Water Gipsy*, in the foreground, and *Niña*, following,
sail with rails awash in a dry squall off Marthas Vineyard during
the New York Yacht Club Cruise of 1936. A sharp gust is keeping crews
busy – especially the bowman on *Water Gipsy* changing down
to a smaller jib.
Water Gipsy, a sixty-footer designed by John Alden and built in 1931,
is a typical American schooner yacht of the nineteen-twenties and
nineteen-thirties – a smaller and sleeker version of the New England
fishing schooners. *Niña* is a departure from the type, designed by Starling
Burgess with an aerodynamic staysail-schooner rig for an owner who
intended to win the 1928 transAtlantic race from New York to Santander,
Spain. *Niña* won that race, beating the big three-masted schooner *Atlantic*,
holder of the transAtlantic speed record since 1905, and she went on
to win the 1928 Fastnet Race too.
Niña was a legendary ocean racer, winning the Bermuda Race in 1962,
thirty-four years after she was launched.

49. Acushla and Istalena III, 1921

The New York Yacht Club fifty-footers were designed by Nat Herreshoff
for the N.Y.Y.C. as a one-design class intended to be cheap to build,
simple to handle, and very fast. At fifty feet on the waterline,
seventy-two feet on the deck, they were a very larg class
of U.S. one-designs – but not the largest, an honor that belongs
to the New York Yacht Club 70s, seen in photo 40.
Nine N.Y.Y.C. fifties were built, beginning in 1913.
At least by the standards of the time, the rig was very simple:
no bowsprit and just two jibs, the larger equipped with a boom
and therefore self-tacking, the other a small flying jib.
The big mainsail was accompanied by a gaff-topsail.
This rig could be handled by a small crew made up of a professional
captain and two sailors. There was also a steward to wait on the owner.
Some examples of this class are still sailing the waters off the U.S. East
Coast, although their rigging has been modified. Nowadays, no mere
three men would want to handle such a "simple" arrangement of sails.

50. Fogbound, 1954

Five yachts, each different, but all 7/8 rigged, are typical of the cruising-racing family boats of the 1950s. In the calm waters of an anchorage in Fishers Island Sound, the boats are waiting for the morning fog to lift before beginning a day of racing. They are anchored side by side in groups of five, both to save space in the bay and to avoid troublesome entanglements during the night, when wind shifts can make boats turn on their anchors.

The atmosphere is serene and cozy, inspiring a reserved, sympathetic camaraderie that yachting teaches. It is agreeable for crews to meet again in the morning after a night sleeping on board, exchanging greetings from cockpit to cockpit, with recollections of the previous evening's fun, and anticipation of the new day's racing. Sailors of the time – a period continuing into the sixties and seventies – typically sailed, competed, slept – in short, lived – on board their boats during race weeks or weekends.

51. Cotton Blossom III, 1941

In 1942 the last American J-Class yacht was broken up, sacrificing its materials to the war effort. After the war, in a different time for yacht racing and much else, big and disposable yachts like the Js were too great an extravagance, and racing for the America's Cup would resume in a class of yachts half the size of the great J-boats: the International Rating twelve meters.

The first American twelve-meter yacht, designed by Starling Burgess, was the 1928 *Waiandance*, sail number US 1. Along with five other twelve-meters designed by Burgess, *Waiandance* was built by Abeking & Rasmussen in Germany. Rosenfeld's photo captures her driving powerfully to windward in 1941, after a name change to *Cotton Blossom III*. Following the six Burgess boats of 1928, at least forty-nine more U.S. twelve-meter yachts were built, many of them for America's Cup competition. The 1987 *Stars and Stripes* bears the number US 55.

52. Tanya II, ca. 1950

When your crew is skilled, reliable and perhaps above all muscular, you can let yourself have some fun. So hoist the spinnaker! Surfing down a wave, the big sail begins to pull. In the cockpit all eyes are on the spinnaker while hands are ready to haul the sheet at the slightest hint of a luff: the helmsman feels the tiller beginning to vibrate, and must be ready to react if the boat threatens to yaw. The helmsman may be asking the crew to make some adjustments: get the jib in, raise the spinnaker pole, haul taut, square away the mainsail, let out half a meter of halyard.

Tanya II is an old boat that had been given radical rebuilding. She had been built in 1927 to a design by Charles Mower and was originally yawl-rigged, but was rebuilt in 1941 and fitted out as a sloop.

53. Members of the N.Y.Y.C. Race Committee, 1978

When *Australia II*, with John Bertrand at the helm, won the seventh race against Dennis Conner's *Liberty* in the summer of 1983, it wiped these slightly arrogant smiles off the faces of the New York Yacht Club Race Committee forever.

We hope and trust that the America's Cup will be sailed for another hundred years and more; but we may never again see these gentlemen, in their blazers and straw hats, watching the stubborn efforts of upstart challengers with quite the same smug attitude as before.

And this is a bit sad.

It was certainly part of the event's fascination that an outcome favorable to the challenger seemed impossible. In every sport, in every race, there is always a favorite, and the favorite is often the underdog. And sometimes such an outsider wins. But not in the America's Cup. The winner, as the members of the New York Yacht Club Race Committee were well aware, was going to be the Cup's defender. Until 1983.

54. Loftsman Paul Coble at Minneford Yacht Yard, ca. 1963

Before the computer age, the inner sanctum of a shipyard was the loft floor; and the loftsman was a sorcerer presiding over some of the most important rites involved in building a yacht or ship. The loftsman transferred to a 1:1 scale (i.e., full-size) the plans for the shape of the hull. The ease or difficulty, success or failure, of building the hull in the shape intended by the designer depended upon the loftsman's skill in getting the lines right.

On the loft floor of the Minneford Yacht Yard in City Island, New York, a new twelve-meter is coming into being. Since the photo dates from 1963, the yacht is probably *Constellation*, the new twelve designed by Olin Stephens for the 1964 America's Cup.

Minneford's has built other Cup defenders. After *Constellation*, the yard built the Stephens-designed *Intrepid*, perhaps the most glorious of all twelve-meter boats, which defended the Cup in 1967 and again in 1970. There followed *Courageous*, *Enterprise*, and *Freedom*, all from Olin Stephens, as well as *Independence*, designed by Ted Hood in 1977.

55. Stevens Institute, 1958

A famous contemporary skipper claims that "the America's Cup is won with just three ingredients: the helmsman, the sails, and the rules." This was true at Cowes in the summer of 1851, and it continued to hold good for the twenty-five challenges that were sailed between 1870 and 1983.

Once the Americans had carried the hundred-guinea cup home to the New York Yacht Club, they wrote rules for subsequent challenges – the famous Deed of Gift – that placed challengers under particular handicaps. But rules apart, it was their technical approach to yacht racing at this highest level that continued to give them an advantage in this fascinating contest.

This is well-illustrated by the photo of three technicians of the Stevens Institute of Technology intently studying four models of America's Cup boats, twelve-meter hulls ready for trials in the testing tank. For decades, this type of testing formed the basis for every improvement in hull performance in the twelve-meter era of the America's Cup.

Only the advent of the computer was to render the trial of models in the waters of the tank obsolete (although not completely).

56. Reliance, 1903

Reliance, the American defender for the 1903 challenge, represented the most extreme point in the evolution of large racing yachts prior to the limitations imposed by the formulas introduced at the beginning of the century – the Universal Rule in the U.S. and the International Rule in Europe – both formulas intended not only to make yacht racing more fair, but to make yachts less freakish. These design and rating rules used length at the waterline as part of their calculations – but obviously measured with the boat not in motion. Designers, well aware that waterline length determines the maximum speed achievable by a boat, accordingly designed slim hulls with extremely long overhangs, so that the length at the waterline would increase just as soon as the boat heeled by even a few degrees.

Reliance was the most extreme of these turn-of-the-century types. At anchor, her length at the waterline was a few inches under 90 feet; but overall length exceeded 143 feet! She carried more than 16,000 square feet of sail – more sail on a single mast than had ever been spread before! All this sail was balanced by a hundred tons of lead in her carefully shaped keel.

Her hull plating was bronze over a frame of steel, and her deck was made of aluminum covered with cork for better traction. The machinery for handling sheets and halyards was all below decks; the topmast could telescope into the mast to reduce the weight in a stiff wind; and the hollow rudder was filled with oil at high speeds, so as to shift the weight astern.

57. Ranger's interior, 1937

Although the J-boats were nothing but racing machines, the rules required them to have a certain minimum of interior furnishing. The forward portion of the hull, housing a sail bin as well as the galley and the crew's quarters, was as Spartan as could be.

But the owner's quarters aft managed a certain decorum, imitating in their furnishings and finishings the style of the great yachts of the period. But here the construction accommodated the need to save weight above the waterline as much as possible. Partitions were of light veneered materials, decorative moldings were kept to a minimum, and everything unnecessary was eliminated.

Still we should not be surprised at the presence here of two items that today would be considered unusual aboard a yacht: the fireplace and the Oriental carpet. The first heated a space which was cool and damp a lot of the time. The second was a stylish touch that Mr. and Mrs. Vanderbilt must have appreciated – as we do, too, looking at this photo.

58. Ranger's interior, 1937
This is the cabin of Mr. and Mrs. Vanderbilt aboard *Ranger*, although
I don't think the owners ever slept here, since *Ranger* was always escorted
by *Vara*, the family's big diesel yacht. While these quarters have been
shaped by the need for lightness, they are nonetheless extraordinarily
elegant. The moldings of the woodwork are slender but beautifully
geometrical. The upholstery of the beds is simple yet graceful,
with scalloped bedspreads that hang down to double as coverings
for the back rests of the couches.
Then there is the table, an item not usually found in a sleeping space.
Here, however, given the lack of a saloon (sacrificed to other more pressing
necessities), it fits in with no difficulty. This table obviously swings
in order to remain level: a feature that modern yachts, for some mysterious
reason, seem to have increasingly abandoned. At the head of the table
is a container for two bottles and an ice bucket.
Today, we deeply regret to say, none of this remains. Of the twelve J-boats
constructed around the world, the only ones left are the British boats
Shamrock V, *Endeavour I*, and *Velsheda*, all heavily remodeled.
The second *Endeavour* and the six American boats – *Yankee*, *Weetamoe*,
Whirlwind, *Enterprise*, *Rainbow*, and *Ranger* – were broken up long ago.

59. Shamrock IV, 1920
As an example of the New York Yacht Club's attitude toward the Cup,
it is worth recalling the story of the fourth challenge presented by Sir
Thomas Lipton.
Following the 1903 Cup series won by the freakish *Reliance*, the N.Y.Y.C.
commissioned Nat Herreshoff to work out a rating formula and had
adopted his Universal Rule that encouraged more wholesome racing
yachts and designated classes by assigning them letters of the alphabet.
Lipton, glad not to have to build a new useless monster (which is what
the previous America's Cup contenders had been) launched a new
challenge with a proposed J-Class yacht. Twice, in 1907 and 1912,
the New York Yacht Club refused to take up his challenge, claiming that, as
a special event, the Cup was not necessarily subject to the very rules
promoted by the Club itself! They changed their mind in 1913, upon
receiving yet another challenge from Lipton. Lipton's *Shamrock IV* was
a yacht of J-Class size and other specifications, and *Resolute*, her opponent,
was similar. However, neither were officially J-boats, and the 1920
America's Cup series was still sailed with time allowances (for *Resolute*!)
rather than with yachts evenly matched.
Lipton commissioned Charles E. Nicholson to design *Shamrock IV*.
The designer himself called her an "ugly duckling," and she was certainly
the least graceful America's Cup contender in history. *Shamrock IV* crossed
the ocean under her own power in 1914, but the outbreak of World War
I led to the contest being put off until 1920, when Lipton's yacht faced
Resolute, another Nat Herreshoff design. *Shamrock* did well in the closest
Cup series sailed up to that time – winning the first two races,
one by default and one by good sailing. Nevertheless, the Americans won
the final three races and the series.

60. Shamrock V's interior, 1930
The interior furnishings of the J-Class yachts were limited to the owner's
quarters aft. Other typical characteristics of these advanced yachts were
sail-handling from below decks, special bins for sheets and sails,
and the exposed framing of the hull, visible here.
In the foreground of the photo, we see the machinery for maneuvering
the centerboard that was one of *Shamrock V*'s outstanding features,
and behind these the large two-speed winch for the mainsail halyard.
Other halyards are also led below, and an effort has obviously been made
to place as much weight as possible as low as possible in the hull.
When we compare this photo with others showing the interior
of *Shamrock*'s adversary *Enterprise*, we note that the Americans have taken
a more scientific approach to weight reduction. The planks of the sole are
separated from one another by spaces, much like the floorboards
of a small boat, and the framing is already of an aeronautical sort.
Shamrock V was planked in teak over steel frames, a "composite" form
of shipbuilding and yachtbuilding. *Enterprise* was given bronze plating
over steel frames.

61. Sir Thomas Lipton, 1920
Only since the Second World War have America's Cup challenges become
contests between clubs rather than duels involving some of the great men
of sailing and business. Until 1937, the competition was marked, above all,
by the presence of individuals and dynasties of great wealth. The Morgans
in the late nineteenth century and the Vanderbilts in the twentieth
organized America's Cup defenses against the ambitions first of Lord
Dunraven and then of Thomas Lipton and T.O.M. Sopwith. Of all these
figures, the most familiar of the British America's Cup challengers
is Sir Thomas Lipton.
Of humble Scottish-Irish origins, he had become enormously rich
in the grocery business and by selling the tea that still bears his name.
His success story, along with his jovial character and astonishing tenacity,
was very attractive to Americans. He was less attractive to the British
yachting establishment – being a commoner, however successful,
and a Glasgow-born Scot with Irish-born working-class parents.
His application to the very exclusive Royal Yacht Squadron was discreetly
turned down, despite its having been presented by His Majesty King
Edward VII himself.

62. Weetamoe, 1930

Some of the J-Class yachts launched for the America's Cup never had the honor of taking part in it. One of these was *Weetamoe*, named for a legendary American Indian woman, built to an extremely beautiful design by Clinton Crane, and intended for the defense of the Cup in 1930. Others that never got to participate in 1930 were *Yankee*, the heavy-weather powerhouse designed by Frank Paine, and Francis Herreshoff's *Whirlwind* with her canoe stern and streamlined house structures. The New York Yacht Club's choice was Harold Vanderbilt's *Enterprise*, which easily defended the America's Cup in the series of 1930.

Like *Yankee*, *Weetamoe* tried again in 1934, when the N.Y.Y.C. chose Vanderbilt's *Rainbow*, and once more in 1937, when the choice was Vanderbilt's incomparable *Ranger*. Clinton Crane's design, commissioned by Junius S. Morgan and George Nichols, was nonetheless very competitive. In 1936, a year in which no America's Cup events were held, *Weetamoe* won three times against *Rainbow* and *Yankee* in other races.

63. America, 1893

The schooner yacht *America* was the work of a young New York designer, George Steers, a specialist in schooner-rigged pilot boats who had already distinguished himself by modeling fast yachts for three members of the New York Yacht Club. Steers, who had a solid background in mathematics and technical drawing, designed a hull of slightly over thirty meters, with a sailplan of crisp sails on raked masts that astonished *America*'s British rivals at Cowes in 1851.

The photographer, James Burton, whose collection of glass plates the Rosenfelds acquired, took this portrait of *America* in 1893, more than forty years after she was launched. In the meantime the yacht had spent about ten years in Europe with different owners and had been a Confederate blockade runner during the Civil War, ending up as the property of General Benjamin Butler, who took her cruising and racing until 1901, after changing the color of the hull from black to white (as seen in the photo) and modifying both her hull and her rig. This historic American yacht came to a curious end in 1942, when the roof of the shed where she was stored collapsed under the weight of an exceptional snowfall.

64. Vanitie, 1914

In 1913, ten years after his defeat by *Reliance* in 1903, Sir Thomas Lipton made plans to return to the United States, this time with a fourth *Shamrock*, a racing yacht of 75 feet waterline length designed by Charles Nicholson to roughly the same dimensions and Universal-Rule specifications that her American adversary would have.

Nevertheless, neither *Shamrock IV* or *Resolute*, the N.Y.Y.C. defender in 1920, were officially J-boats. The 1920 Cup series still involved handicapping — in *Resolute*'s case a seven-minute time allowance over Lipton's fourth *Shamrock*. The first official J-boat was *Shamrock V* of 1930. And what of *Vanitie*, the lovely big yacht shown in silhouette here? She was a candidate for the honor of defending the Cup in the 1914 series that was delayed for six years by World War I.

Designed by William Gardner of New York, who created the great *Atlantic*, *Vanitie* for all her beauty would have run serious risks against Lipton's "ugly duckling," *Shamrock IV*.

As events played out, *Shamrock* remained on the American side of the ocean and in 1920 challenged the Herreshoff-designed *Resolute*. Lipton's fourth *Shamrock* badly frightened the N.Y.Y.C. when she won the first two races of the 1920 series, although the final result was three to two for the Americans.

65. Yankee, 1937

Yankee, the Boston boat designed by Frank Paine, and nearly selected to defend the America's Cup in the summer of 1934, was active all during the 1930s in Cup-defense trials and in other American versions of England's "Big Class" racing, such as the New York Yacht Club Cruise. She is seen here sporting a new deck arrangement with a rather prominent deckhouse, in front of which there are several decklights — evidence of an effort to confer something of a pleasure-sailing character upon this racing thoroughbred.

The crew, however, is still a large one. The rig is too demanding to permit easy handling, while the hull has too much brute force to be suitable for a relaxed cruise. Soon to replace the jib, the spinnaker is up on the halyard, stopped but ready to go, and the men are mentally rehearsing the tasks to be performed upon reaching the buoy. This boat's power when sailing close-hauled was extraordinary, and this photo gives us a dramatic vision of it.

66. Gretel, 1962

The twelve-meter era of the America's Cup, between 1958 and 1987, brought the contest the agility of this smaller yacht in contrast to the sheer power of the Js. In twelve-meter match racing, what matters more than the speed of the boat as such is its capacity for acceleration: i.e., its ability to pick up speed quickly after coming about, and how quickly the crew can manage the tack itself. Twelve-meter boats are just plain quick. Aboard them, one frequently feels a sort of jolt as soon as the mainsail has been hauled taut. The boat picks up speed like a Flying Dutchman – but the difference is that a twelve-meter weighs about twenty-seven tons! This enormous reserve of "horsepower" in the sails is clear in Stanley Rosenfeld's photo of the 1962 Australian challenger *Gretel* as she takes off under a big spinnaker and, with the help of two cresting waves, surfs to catch up with the American twelve-meter *Weatherly*. She did catch up, too, and went on to win the second race of the series. Designed by Alan Payne, *Gretel* succeeded in defeating *Weatherly* this once, but in the end lost 4-1.

67. Gretel, 1962

Here is another dramatic photo from the 1962 twelve-meter America's Cup duels between Australia's *Gretel* and America's *Weatherly* – this one taken on the first leg of the same race as the photo to the left. After eight miles of beating into a good breeze and a choppy sea, only one boat lenght separates *Gretel* from *Weatherly* as the two yachts round the mark. Here *Gretel*'s crew puts weight on the windward rail as they fight to catch up with the Americans.

68. Columbia and Shamrock, 1899

At the end of the last century, America's Cup contenders belonged to what the British correctly called the Big Class – yachts whose unprecedented lengths approached forty meters, with towering sailplans to match. The 1899 challenge saw the emergence of a man whose purse and personality would be linked to the next five Cup challenges: Sir Thomas Lipton. The first of his five *Shamrocks* was designed by William Fife, Jr., a descendent of the famous Scottish shipbuilding family from the Clyde. This first *Shamrock* had an overall length of thirty-nine meters and twenty-seven at the waterline, with a six-meter draft to offset the weight of the gigantic steel mast that carried the sails to an altitude of forty-two meters above the deck. The hull was sheathed in a bronze-manganese alloy that prevented the growth of marine organisms and could be polished as smooth as glass.
But Fife's *Shamrock* had to face *Columbia*, an even more extreme design by Nat Herreshoff: bronze sheathing, a steel skeleton, a completely empty interior. *Shamrock* lost three races out of three and the Cup remained at the New York Yacht Club. Lipton, however, was seduced by the challenge and glamour of these races and would return in 1901.

69. Zio and Nightwind, 1939

By the end of the thirties, there was a fleet of twelve-meter yachts racing in America, joining the even larger fleet of six-meters that had come along since the early 1920s. The first American to take on the challenge of designing twelves to Europe's meter-boat formulas was Starling Burgess who, in 1928, had six such boats built by Abeking & Rasmussen in Germany, a legendary yachtbuilder well acquainted with this class. These were the first six twelves to bear numbers preceded by the letters US. The year 1930 saw the importation of an old Norwegian twelve-meter named *Magda XI*, which became *Cantitoe*, number US7. And between 1925 and 1939 were built *Seven Seas*, US9, designed by Clinton Crane and built by Nevins; Francis Herreshoff's *Mitena*, US10; *Gleam*, US11, also by Clinton Crane and Nevins; and the first three twelve-meter designs by Olin Stevens, likewise built by Nevins: *Nyala*, *Northern Light*, and *Vim*, respectively numbers US12, US14, US15. *Zio* and *Nightwind* are US8 and US13. This is a classic Rosenfeld photo that represents both sailing power and literally the "design" of a photographic image.

70. Ranger, 1937

Ranger's mainsail is made up of something like four hundred seventy square meters of Egyptian cotton: almost a ton of canvas to be hoisted by sheer muscle power! And then there is the friction of the sail guides in the mast slot: guides that a sailor, suspended in a boatswain's chair, with his feet braced against the mast, has to align one by one as the sail rises. Fortunately – but only for this particular task – the day doesn't seem to offer much of a breeze. Those of us who have had similar experiences on board a modern sixty-footer can only imagine what it must have been like trying to hoist *Ranger's* mainsail when there was a wind, with a twenty-one meter boom moving back and forth at head height and the canvas snapping violently – all of this in the tense atmosphere preceding an America's Cup race! There are sixteen sailors visibly involved in this task, plus, undoubtedly, a few others outside the picture frame. It took practically the entire crew to carry out this maneuver that, luckily, took place only at the start of the race, since the J-Class boats didn't reef their sails.

They had no need to do so, since Cup rules only permitted them to race in winds of under twenty-one knots. Under that limit, their ballast of a hundred and more tons of lead was sufficient to balance the heeling power of their huge mainsails. And winds of under twenty-one knots were sufficient to move them with the power and drama we see here in J-Class photos.

71. Ranger, 1937

On a J-Class yacht, tacking called for muscle, timing, and mechanical advantage. The sheets of the sails at the bow – one from the foresail and two from the large trapezoidal jib – were controlled from capstans or winches on deck, as were sheets for the flying sails and, astern, the mainsail sheet. The winches on *Ranger* were of two basic types. The large "coffee-grinder" amidships needed four men to work it, plus a fifth to take up the line moving through. The other winches or capstans, like the one in the photo, employed three crew. In addition to the running rigging, every tack demanded a mechanical adjustment of the curve of the long and flexible boom to obtain the best aerodynamic shape for the mainsail.

These crewmen aboard the great *Ranger* are dressed like U.S. Navy sailors – professionals in white uniforms and sailor caps. The skilled amateurs who would crew aboard the twelve-meters from the 1950s to the 1980s would dress in shorts and jerseys like the sportsmen they were.

72. Gleam, 1955

The eleventh U.S. twelve-meter, *Gleam* was designed by Clinton Crane and built by the Nevins yacht yard of City Island, New York City, in 1937. Here she is eighteen years later during an afternoon sail on Long Island Sound. A crewman has gone overboard and has been retrieved on this calm day. Everyone seems to be amused. *Gleam* is one of the twelve-meter survivors, now restored and sailing out of Newport, Rhode Island, the perfect home port for an antique racing yacht of her grace and pedigree!

73. Weatherly, 1961

Sailing on board a twelve-meter in a stiff wind is definitely a sporting activity. The boat is lively, and every maneuver demands a physical effort and equally quick reaction. Another outstanding characteristic of a sail on the deck of a twelve-meter is the ease with which one can get drenched, since this type of yacht seems to be designed for running straight into a wave and throwing up lots of spray.

The twelve-meter era of the America's Cup, following the extravagant J-boat era before the war, began in 1958. The first to resume challenges for the America's Cup in the years after the war were, naturally, the English. Their cousins on the American side responded as they always had, organizing very tough elimination races and crew-training sails. One of the most tenacious defense candidates was *Weatherly*, whose crew at the coffee-grinder is here seen during an especially demanding training sail. Designed by Phil Rhodes and built in 1958 by Luders Marine, *Weatherly* was bested in the elimination trials by the Olin-Stephens - designed *Columbia*. But *Weatherly* came back for the Cup series of 1962, being chosen to defend and beating the Australian challenger *Gretel* 4-1.

74. Rainbow, 1934

The sailors on board America's Cup defenders before the 1950s
were mostly salaried employees who lived with the yacht through
a long season of training and fine-tuning, elimination trials and – in the
event of being chosen to defend by the New York Yacht Club – Cup races.
Not much as been written about the sailors of these yachts,
and photographs of them are even rarer. We know little about how
they were organized for the sophisticated sailing they were to do as a team,
how technically skilled they were, or how they were chosen.
We do know that a J-Class yacht carried around thirty professional sailors
who had to train hard, repeating maneuvers until they achieved
near-perfect synchronization, speed, and skill. When they weren't involved
in handling the vessel, their life on board was far less glamorous
than images of these J-Class racing machines might suggest, since the J-Class
yachts of 1930s America's Cup racing were very spare and businesslike
below decks. The sailors slept on canvas bunks that were folded against
the raw sides of the hull during the day to get them out of the way.
They ate off folding tables in the same quarters. For Cup races,
all these amenities were left ashore. The only luxury left was the cook,
probably the gentleman with the bow tie and the hard stare.

75. Reliance, 1903

The photo is by James Burton, a colleague of Morris Rosenfeld's.
Reliance's deck is shown in all its racing-machine complexity.
In the foreground appears an enormous boom of around twenty-five
meters, belonging to the balloon jib, which was the ancestor
of the spinnaker.
Right behind it is the double helm, with the incomparable Charlie Barr
steering. *Reliance* must have been particularly hard to steer when heeled,
and this must be why Herreshoff equipped the wheel with a brake pedal
that the helmsman could use to hold the helm and allow himself
a few moments' rest. The helmsman also benefited from an indicator
that told him the exact angle of the rudder.
The sailors are all lying flat on the deck, with the weight of their bodies
as far outboard as safety will allow to counterbalance the heeling.
When racing, *Reliance* carried at least twenty-five sailors, whose collective
weight totaled around two tons. Near the helmsman, there were usually
several "advisors": the tactician, the navigator, the designer of the vessel.

76. Easterner, 1972

For the 1958 America's Cup, the first since before World War II,
the Americans designed and built three International Rule twelve-meter
boats: *Columbia*, designed by Olin Stephens; *Weatherly*,
drawn by Phil Rhodes; and *Easterner*. This last was the work of Ray Hunt,
a great sailor much better known now for the deep-vee powerboat hull
adopted around the world during the past four decades.
Easterner was never a real competitor in 1958 – but this historic twelve
is a survivor, still sailing in California under the name of *Newsboy*.
During training sails, maneuvers were repeated and repeated to let
the crew acquire the necessary synchronization and speed.
In America's Cup match racing, a leg sailed close to the wind can call
for as many as twenty or twenty-five tacks. If a boat takes one second more
to tack than its adversary, it can find itself twenty-five seconds behind
at the finish.
But however much you train, something can always go wrong. Here there
seems to be a bit of confusion aloft, where the starboard halyard,
to leeward, left slack, has started misbehaving. The bowman is paying
for this error with some aerial acrobatics; above all, the problem will have
brought with it some loss of concentration on the part of the helmsman
and the rest of the crew.

77. The N.Y.Y.C. Race Committee, 1903

Ever since the schooner *America* carried the hundred-guinea cup home
to the New York Yacht Club, the club and its Race Committee had been
the arbiters of contests that began in 1870 with disadvantaged foreign
challengers attempting to win what became known as the America's Cup.
The New York Yacht Club decided which challenges it would accept
or reject, established the rules that governed the races, decided what type
of boats would be raced, and finally chose the defender from among
a group of good candidates.
This photo is by James Burton – and once more we must express
our gratitude to the Rosenfelds for preserving not only their own images
but also the work of colleagues. Here we see the Race Committee
in July of 1903, during the Cup competition between the N.Y.Y.C.'s
sail-carrying monster *Reliance* and Sir Thomas Lipton's *Shamrock III*.
Consulting a chronometer, they are counting the seconds to the cannon
shot. The committee members are relaxed and almost bored; this time,
as ever, nothing untoward will occur. In the 1903 Cup series, poor
Shamrock never led at any mark.

78. The N.Y.Y.C. America's Cup Committee, 1967

After a century of unfailing victories, the New York Yacht Club
saw America's Cup contests as a social event, a unique sort of "society
regatta" in which the adversary was a foreign yacht club.

It was like a duel between a foreign knight and the champion of the realm,
and the outcome was all but taken for granted. In photos of New York
Yacht Club Race Committees and America's Cup Committees, we see all
the detachment and sense of security of people who know they are
directing a perfectly controlled event on their home territory,
in accordance with rules dictated by themselves.

Viewed from behind on board *Djinn*, a cutter of sixty-two feet belonging
to Henry Morgan – Commodore of the New York Yacht Club – the
committee members are watching one of the American twelve-meters go
by during the races to select the 1967 defender.

For the record, the defender turned out to be *Intrepid*, and she inflicted
a straight series of defeats (4-0) on the challenger *Dame Pattie*, the second
Australian yacht to give the competition a try. *Intrepid's* helmsman was
a legendary figure in America's Cup racing: Emil "Bus" Mosbacher.

79. Endeavour II, 1937

In 1934 there came to the America's Cup a new charismatic challenger,
Thomas Octave Murdoch Sopwith, better known as T.O.M. Sopwith.
He was very much Harold Vanderbilt's English counterpart. Both were
pure amateurs, great enthusiasts and great organizers. Both had their
wives at their side while racing – in Mrs. Sopwith's case as timekeeper.
The builder of the famous Sopwith Camel airplane twice presented
himself as an America's Cup contender, with two J-boats that were
perhaps – the first certainly – the most fearsome adversaries the Americans
had ever faced: *Endeavours I* and *II*, both designed by Charles E. Nicholson
and built of steel at Gosport in the Camper & Nicholson shipyards.
Sopwith proved as skillful a helmsman as Vanderbilt. He had prepared
the first *Endeavour* very well, training against two other British J-Class
yachts, both designed by Nicholson: *Shamrock V*, the last of Lipton's series,
and *Velsheda*, which never left British waters.

But in America he had to fire his crew, who had gone on strike over issues
of pay. In their place he brought aboard British amateurs – sailors who,
while willing enough, were not sufficiently skilled for a Cup series.
Nevertheless they nearly won the Cup in 1934. Sopwith was defeated 4-2,
but it was the closest series in Cup history up to that time.

T.O.M. Sopwith tried again in 1937 with a second *Endeavour*.
The new *Endeavour* was very fast, but not fast enough to beat
the "super J," as Vanderbilt described his *Ranger*.

The faces of Sopwith and his wife betray their disappointment as they
leave *Endeavour II* aboard a Gar Wood speedboat – a very elegant boat,
to be sure, but also very American!

Index

Printed in Italy